The Hand
of the
Holy Spirit

MIRACULOUS ANSWERS
TO PRAYERS

by

Thomas Mark Ziebold

VMI PUBLISHERS

Partnering With Christian Authors, Publishing Christian and Inspirational Books

Sisters, Oregon

Published by

CitadelBooks

a division of VMI Publishers
Sisters, Oregon
www.vmipublishers.com

ISBN: 1-933204-17-6
Library of Congress Control Number: 2005911413

Author Contact:
SpiritHand@hotmail.com

TABLE *of* CONTENTS

PREFACE

My mother's life has been touched on numerous occasions by the hand of the Holy Spirit because she has been blessed with a close relationship with Jesus. I decided to write this book to give glory to God for the awesome things he has done in her life. I believe these stories must be passed on to other Christians and to non-believers so that they can understand there is a God and that he is an awesome God who still performs miracles today! The Bible provides a few verses in the book of Deuteronomy that tell us how important it is to pass along to our children the stories of the Bible and the miracles that God has performed.

Deuteronomy 11:2-3 says the following:

> [2]*Remember today that your children were not the ones who saw and experienced the discipline of the LORD your God: his majesty, his mighty hand, his outstretched arm;*[3] *the signs he performed and the things he did in the heart of Egypt, both to Pharaoh king of Egypt and to his whole country.*

This verse holds so much meaning for me. None of us has a firsthand account of what happened in the heart of Egypt or of the miracles that God performed there. The Bible has documented these miraculous events, but it is our responsibility to pass this knowledge on to our children and future generations.

Christians have an important responsibility to share the accounts and events that have been told in the Bible to future generations, so that all of mankind can benefit from God's miraculous acts.

Deuteronomy 11:18-19 says the following:

> [18]*Fix these words of mine in your hearts and minds; tie them as symbols on your hands and bind them on your foreheads.* [19]*Teach them to your children, talking about them when you sit at home and when you walk along the road, when you lie down and when you get up.*

This book is written as an autobiography from my mother's point of view. The organization of the book is in somewhat of a chronological order, but a few events are presented out of chronologic order. This has been done in order to make the overall flow of the book a bit more logical. It's important for the reader to understand that the book is a compilation of the events in my mother's life during which she felt the most direct interaction with the Holy Spirit. The chapters are organized to present spiritual "snapshots" into her life, but the chapters aren't necessarily dependent upon each other. The book is best read if the reader views each chapter as its own independent event within her life and doesn't try to figure out how all of the chapters fit together in a chronological timeline.

I have written this book because I think it's important that people understand that the God in the Bible, the God of miracles, is the same God we serve today. He has never changed, and he continues to look after his followers. God performs miracles on their behalf. Furthermore, he desires to have a relationship with us, and he runs to greet us with open arms if we take but a single step in his direction. What an awesome God we serve!

My mother and I have dedicated this book to our children and grandchildren. We pray that our children will grow to have a close relationship with Jesus and that they will share the stories of the Bible with future generations.

I firmly believe that this is the most important knowledge that can be passed from generation to generation, and I want my children and grandchildren to know what an awesome relationship my mom has with Jesus and the miraculous events he has performed in her life.

The CONVERSION *of* MY FATHER

My father was an extremely caring and loving man. He had a generous and loving heart but had a tendency to be a bit timid. He couldn't bear to see anyone suffer and, as a result, oftentimes encountered difficulty in his position as a manager and landlord of the apartment buildings he owned. He found it hard to confront the employees he managed or lessees who were not paying their rent on time. My mother, on the other hand, was a very strong-willed person. She had a difficult time understanding why my father had such a timid personality. As a result, she had a tendency to place a lot of added pressure on my father. My father's inability to cope well with this pressure made it difficult for him to keep his emotions in check.

For a period of time, his doctor prescribed all sorts of medication to help him control his emotions. In fact, my father became completely dependent on these prescription drugs. I can remember times when I was growing up that my father had trays full of prescription medications (depressants and stimulants). His dependence on these medications had a noticeable effect on him physically. For much of his life his hands would shake uncontrollably. I was concerned for my father's health, and it worried me quite a bit.

Eventually, my father lost his job in upper management. This turned out to be somewhat beneficial for him, however, because my sister Paula was married to the son of a Baptist pastor at the time. After my father lost his job, the pastor would find building projects and renovation projects that needed to be done within the church. This enabled my father to receive an income for the work he performed and provided an opportunity for the pastor to witness to my father about Jesus while he was working. I had no idea the pastor was witnessing to my father, but I later found that the message was having a dramatic effect on him.

One day, when I went over to visit my parents, I found my father pouring all of his medications down the toilet. I thought this was going to be a problem because he needed them. I ran over and asked him what he thought he was doing. My father replied that he didn't need the medications any longer. I thought he was crazy! I tried to stop him from pouring all of his medications down the toilet. My father and I struggled for several minutes, and then he looked at me and said, "Pam, I don't need these any longer. I have been saved by Jesus and have been completely converted and healed. I don't need these any longer in my life." He then grabbed me and asked me to take a good look at him. He held his hands straight out in front of him. His hands were as steady as a rock. It was unbelievable for me to see my father as steady as he was at that moment in his life. I had never seen him that steady.

My father finished pouring the medications down the toilet. He had been cured from his dependence on prescribed medications in a single day! This was the first impression I had of the power of the Holy Spirit and his ability to heal lives. It truly had a lasting impression on me.

The BIRTH *of* MY CHILDREN

When I was about thirteen or fourteen I started having many "female" problems. I had repeated visits with many gynecologists and specialists. When I was a junior or senior in high school I was told that it would be impossible for me to ever have children. The doctors recommended several times that I have a complete hysterectomy. They thought that this was my best course of action. They decided that a total hysterectomy would cure the problems I was having, and that I would be much healthier. I was extremely reluctant, however, because I was very young and I always dreamed of having children of my own some day. A total hysterectomy would mean that I could never have children, and I wasn't able to accept that. The doctors understood how drastic this measure was, but they firmly believed it was impossible for me to become pregnant. To them it seemed the most logical course of action. I, however, never could agree to the hysterectomy. It was simply too difficult for me to give up my dreams of having my own children.

I always had a very close relationship with my younger cousin Debbie. Debbie was about six years younger than I, but she loved to tag around with my husband Mark and me. She seemed to really enjoy the time she spent with us and told me on several occasions that she felt Mark and I made a great couple. Debbie had a hard time understanding why we weren't having children of our own. She thought that Mark and I would really make great parents! She finally asked me one day why Mark and I had never had children of our own. I told her I had tremendous "female" problems and that the doctors had told me that it would be impossible for me to have children. At the time, Debbie was young, perhaps a junior in high school. She was attending a Catholic church. Debbie told me that she would pray to St. Jude on my behalf. She told me that St. Jude was the saint of hopeless causes and that he could make it possible for Mark and me to have a child.

I laughed about it, but I let Debbie go ahead and pray to St. Jude on my behalf. At this time I wasn't a Christian, but I didn't want to disappoint her. Debbie prayed to St. Jude, and it wasn't very long after that I thought I became pregnant. I made a visit with my doctor and informed him that I felt I was pregnant. My doctor laughed at me, and said, "Now, Pam, you know that's impossible. You can't have children." He initially told me that it was impossible and that he would see me in about a month — at the time of our next scheduled visit. When I went to leave his office, however, he stopped me and said that he might as well start me on some medication right away. He changed his mind about waiting for our next scheduled visit, because it was obvious that I wasn't feeling "normal." He knew me well enough to know that I wasn't comfortable with his decision to wait a month to see me again, and he decided it made sense to examine me immediately, start me on medication, and then check me again in a month. I remember sitting in the waiting room after his examination. I was wondering what type of medication he might prescribe for me, or if I would require surgery.

I had a lot of thoughts going through my mind. When he finally informed me of the results of my examination he told me that, from what he could tell, it looked like I was pregnant!

He asked me not to share this news with anyone in the family, however, because he still believed it was impossible for me to become pregnant. He wanted to send the lab work out to have it verified. He also indicated that even if I was pregnant, I more than likely would not be able to carry the baby to full term and would likely lose it. He said it was best not to share the news with anyone else in the family because it might bring disappointment. Hearing that I most likely would lose the baby was discouraging news to me, but I was so excited to finally be pregnant!

I, of course, didn't follow any of his advice. I was so excited that I told everyone in the family the news that I was pregnant. I later found out that, not only was I pregnant, I was pregnant with twins, a girl and a boy. I didn't carry the babies to full term, but I did manage to carry them to seven months. Tom and Tami were born on the 4th of December 1969. They were both beautiful, healthy babies. Well, that's not exactly true; Tom was beaten up in the womb pretty badly by his sister. His face was bruised and battered.

In fact, it was so bad that my father went down to the hospital chapel to pray for him as soon as possible after his birth. The doctors indicated, however, that babies' faces were still quite "pliable" and that the face could be massaged into the proper form and that the bruises would heal. They were right, because after massaging Tom's head and face for several days, he was just as beautiful as any other baby in the nursery. The twins were a little small, but that was to be expected for twins that were carried for only seven months.

To this day I firmly believe that the birth of the twins was a gift from God. I believe the birth came as a direct result of the prayers from Debbie. Even though she was praying to St. Jude, I think that, in her heart, she was really praying to Jesus, and it was through these prayers that I was permitted to give birth to twins. I thank Jesus every night for my children. I don't know what he has in store for their lives but I firmly believe they are gifts from God and their birth was a miraculous event in my life.

MY
CONVERSION

My mother and father were Methodist, and we attended church on a fairly regular basis. I was very active in church during my childhood. I was a member of the youth group and participated in most of the church activities. Despite attending church on a regular basis, I was never given the opportunity to witness someone trusting Jesus and committing his or her life to serving him. Our church was very private, and most people involved in our church kept many aspects of their walk with Jesus to themselves. As a result, I never had the opportunity to witness how Jesus worked within the lives of Christians on a daily basis. Also, despite being very active in church, I didn't study my Bible on a consistent basis and didn't know it very well. As a young person, I guess I just didn't feel the need to study the Bible and I didn't take the time necessary to understand God's Word. I'm extremely grateful that my parents raised me in church. Being raised in church gave me a foundation in Christianity that I later fell back on when times got really difficult in my life. Parents should always remember that they have a responsibility to raise their children to know Jesus. Proverbs 22:6 (NLT) says, "Teach your children to choose the right path, and when they are older, they will remain upon it."

It's important to remember this Bible verse even when it seems your children aren't getting the message, or aren't listening to what you have to say. Oftentimes the foundation that is laid at an early age becomes important later in life. In my personal life this was certainly the case.

By the time I was eighteen years old, church no longer seemed important in my life. I was an adult and I thought I was so smart and grown up that I didn't need an active church life any longer. I continued to pray, however, and always felt that I had a close relationship with Jesus. It was during this time in my life that I started to experiment with other belief systems. I became a follower of Edgar Casey. I believed in the idea of reincarnation. I visited fortunetellers and played games with the Ouija board. Since I had never really read the Bible, I had no idea that what I was doing was contradictory to God's word. I had no idea that my relationship with Jesus was being attacked by other belief systems that I had allowed into my life. As Christians we need to understand that it is very important to remain active in church and to understand and read the Bible. Our lives can be attacked by the powers of evil without our knowledge. We can be led down the wrong path quietly and subtly without knowing that what we are doing is contradictory to a walk with Jesus. The evil one often uses subtle and quiet attacks against us to lead us away from Jesus. If we don't have a full understanding of the Bible we can quickly become vulnerable to these subtle attacks. The Bible warns against this. Hebrews 13:9 (NLT) says, "Do not be attracted by strange, new ideas. Your spiritual strength comes from God's special favor, not from ceremonial rules about food, which don't help those who follow them." And 1 Peter 5:8 says, "Be self-controlled and alert. Your enemy the devil prowls around like a roaring lion looking for someone to devour."

During this time in my life I had been told by several of my Baptist friends that I was going to die and go to hell because I had not entrusted my life to Jesus. My sister Paula started dating the son of a Baptist pastor at about this time. Paula told me that I was destined to die and go to hell unless I gave my life to Jesus Christ. She even tried to drag me down the church aisle on a few occasions in order to get me to turn my life over to Jesus. At the time, I didn't know how important this message was for a number of reasons. First, I wasn't reading my Bible, so I didn't know what was required to turn my life over to Jesus and trust in him for my salvation. Second, I wasn't attending church on a regular basis, so I was no longer having consistent fellowship with other Christians. Third, while all of my friends were witnessing to me, they seemed to be leading hypocritical lives. Many things they were involved in didn't seem to indicate the close walk with Jesus that they were talking about. For all of these reasons, I didn't turn my life over to Jesus at that time. I was, however, hearing the message of salvation so I was gradually becoming aware of what was required to have true salvation through the blood that Jesus shed on the cross.

Soon after our children were born, Mark and I started having severe marital problems. It seemed the added pressure of the children and Mark working long hours for General Motors was too much to bear. Our relationship turned very ugly during these years, and we came very close to divorcing each other. Despite not attending church on a regular basis and not reading my Bible, the Christian foundations had been established in my life at an early age. In addition, I had never stopped praying to Jesus and had always felt I had a close walk with him. It was during these difficult times in my life that I fell back to my Christian roots. I decided that Mark and I should attend marriage counseling. At first Mark didn't feel we needed marriage counseling and was extremely reluctant to the idea. I attended counseling meetings on my own with the pastor I had grown up with at the Methodist church. The counseling sessions helped a little bit, but it was difficult because Mark wouldn't attend them with me. Finally, I suggested that, since Mark and I were of different religious denominations, he should set up an appointment with the Rev. Wesley Poole. Reverend Poole was Mark's cousin, and was a Nazarene pastor. Mark agreed to meet with Wesley, and I agreed to attend the meeting with Mark.

When we arranged to meet with Wesley we didn't provide him with a reason for the meeting. When we arrived at his home Wesley met Mark and shook his hand. Wesley asked Mark if he had felt called to be a pastor. I guess he felt that Mark might be called to be a pastor, since Mark's father had been a dynamic pastor. Mark didn't feel a calling to become a pastor and he told Wesley that he needed some advice and some counseling. It's kind of sad to say, but I remember that I wasn't paying very close attention to what was being said at the counseling session with Wesley. I really had the idea that Mark was the one who really needed the counseling and was the one that was causing most of the problems in our marriage. Looking back on this, I think it was probably a bit selfish to think that he was the one causing all of the problems in our relationship, but that was how I felt at the time. Because I wasn't paying much attention, I allowed my mind to wonder a bit.

While my mind was wondering I began to think about Jesus and my life. Then, quite unexpectedly, I had one of the most awesome experiences in my life. There, in Middletown, Ohio, in Wesley's parlor, I was touched directly by the Holy Spirit. This was the first time I had ever experienced the presence of the Holy Spirit in my life, but he communed with me directly and filled my entire spirit. It was a truly unique and awesome experience that was unmistakable in its importance to my life. He filled my mind and body with his spirit. He told me that he had died on the cross for me and that I could have everlasting life, but that it was only achievable through the blood that was shed on the cross. I suddenly understood the sacrifice that Jesus made on the cross and its importance to my life! I became completely aware of the fact that when Jesus died on that cross he became the perfect sacrificial lamb, and his blood was enough to wash away every sin I had committed in the past, as well as every sin I would ever commit. At that moment in my life I experienced a sudden realization that the only way to achieve my salvation was to believe in Jesus and accept him as my personal savior.

This must have been like Saul's experience when he was knocked off his horse and then converted his life to spreading the message of the resurrection of Jesus. This was no ordinary experience! The Holy Spirit completely filled my soul. While this was going on, Wesley noticed that something extraordinary was occurring within me. Wesley took the opportunity to pray with me, and I bowed my knee and turned my life over to the Holy Spirit that night in his parlor. The following Sunday I attended the service at Wesley's church. When the call came to approach the altar, I went up to the altar and reaffirmed my salvation. I converted my life to serving Jesus, and I have never regretted my decision. This is one of the most awesome experiences I have ever had in my life and it truly turned my life around. Committing my life to serving Jesus entirely changed me as a person.

The Bible makes it clear that when someone trusts Jesus as their savior they become a completely different person. 2 Corinthians 5:17 (NLT) says, "Those who become Christians become new persons. They are not the same anymore, for the old life is gone. A new life has begun."

This experience definitely changed my life and I can say that my life has never been the same since the night I converted my life to serving Jesus. It's difficult for me to put into words the type of feeling I had on that night. I know that I was in direct communion with the Holy Spirit. If you ever have the opportunity to experience this fellowship with the Holy Spirit it is unmistakable! The following verses make it clear that God communes directly with his followers. He grants them wisdom that is beyond mortal understanding:

> *The Lord grants wisdom. From his mouth comes knowledge and understanding. He grants a treasure of good sense to the godly. He is their shield, protecting those who walk with integrity. (Prov. 2:6-7 NLT)*

> *God has actually given us his spirit (not the world's spirit) so we can know the wonderful things God has freely given us. When we tell you this, we do not use words of human wisdom. We speak words given to us by the Spirit, using the Spirit's words to explain spiritual truths.*

> *But people who aren't Christians can't understand these truths from God's spirit. It all sounds foolish to them because only those who have the Spirit can understand what the Spirit means. (1 Cor. 2:12-14 NLT)*

I have no doubt that on that night in Wesley's parlor I was in direct communion with the Holy Spirit. He granted me the wisdom of knowing what I truly needed to do in order to receive my salvation. He also confirmed to me that he had a plan for my life and that it would be achieved only by serving him.

WHITE
LEATHER
SANDALS

While I was living in Cincinnati I became very active in church. Mark drove a bus route through Forest Park in Cincinnati, picking up children to take to church each Sunday. Another member of the church, Mary, and I would walk the bus route, going door to door, asking people if they would send their children to church each week. We invited young people to attend our church services each week. Many of these young people didn't have parents who were active in church, so the only way for them to attend the church services was to ride the church bus.

I had been noticing a pair of white leather sandals at a shoe store near our house. The sandals were beautiful, and I fell in love with them. The only problem was that the sandals were a half size too small for me. For some reason I decided to buy the sandals even though they didn't fit my feet and were uncomfortable. I guess I figured the sandals would eventually stretch to fit my feet because they were leather. One morning, on my way to pick up Mary, I decided to put the sandals in my car. I placed the sandals on the floor in the back seat of my car. To this day I don't know what prompted me to take the sandals along with me. I was already wearing shoes, and I wouldn't have worn the sandals anyway when I was walking the bus route, as they would have been uncomfortable on my feet. At any rate, I decided to take the sandals with me on this particular day.

I picked up Mary and we rode together in my car to the neighborhood that we were going to walk that day. As we were walking the bus route, we came across a house. We asked the lady of the house if she would permit her three children to attend church services by riding the bus. The lady granted permission, but her daughter, who was probably thirteen or fourteen years old, refused to go. She seemed to be embarrassed, so I asked her what she was embarrassed about. The girl said, "I would attend your church services, except that I don't have a pair of good shoes to wear to church. I would be embarrassed to attend church in any of the shoes I have."

At that moment I knew exactly why I had brought those shoes along with me in the car on that particular day. It became clear to me why I had purchased shoes that were a half size too small. Those shoes were never intended for me! They had caught my eye in the shoe store, and the Holy Spirit impressed upon me to buy the shoes even though they didn't fit. I knew that the shoes would be exactly the right size for this girl. I looked down at the girl's feet and asked her what size shoe she wore, even though I already knew the answer to my question. Amazingly, her shoe size was exactly the same size as the white sandals that I had brought with me that day! I knew without a doubt the purpose for those white leather sandals. The Holy Spirit knew what this girl needed before she had even asked for it! I told her that I just happened to have a brand new pair of white leather sandals in my car and that she should consider these a gift from God. The Holy Spirit intended these sandals for her and I was supposed to give them to her. I got the sandals from my car, gave them to the girl, and asked her if she would attend our church services. She said she would.

The little girl and her family regularly attended our church services for quite some time. In fact, they were still attending church on a regular basis after I moved to Michigan. They had become active in all parts of the church service.

James 1:17 says, "Every good and perfect gift is from above, coming down from the Father of the heavenly lights, who does not change like shifting shadows."

Mathew 6:25-30 says the following:

> *Therefore I tell you, do not worry about your life, what you will eat or drink; or about your body, what you will wear. Is not life more important than food, and the body more important than clothes? Look at the birds of the air; they do not sow or reap or store away in barns, and yet your heavenly Father feeds them. Are you not much more valuable than they? Who of you by worrying can add a single hour to his life? And why do you worry about your clothes? See how the lilies of the field grow. They do not labor or spin. Yet I tell you that not even Solomon in all his splendor was dressed like one of these. If that is how God clothes the grass of the field, which is here today and tomorrow is thrown into the fire, will he not much more clothe you, O you of little faith?*

God provides for his people. He knows their needs before they even ask for them. Oftentimes he has already provided for their need before they even know about it!

MARK'S HAND

When Mark came home from work one night, I could tell something was wrong. It turned out he had been involved in an accident at work. He was working for a General Motors assembly plant that was experiencing all sorts of labor disputes between the union workers and the company. Mark's job as an assembly line supervisor was to make sure that the assembly process ran as smoothly as possible. So the labor dispute made his job extremely difficult. That night one of his workers shut down a conveyor belt in order to cause the seats to back up into each other. Mark realized what had happened and attempted to fix the problem by trying to restart the conveyor. He braced his left hand on a conveyor belt and flipped the switch to restart the assembly process. When the assembly process started, however, Mark could feel his left hand get sucked between the metal rollers of the conveyor belt. He quickly reached up and threw the switch to stop the assembly process but it was too late. The rollers came to a stop about three inches above his wrist. His hand was crushed between the rollers.

Mark said the pain was so severe that he had almost lost consciousness. Had he lost consciousness with his hand caught in the conveyor, he probably would have broken his hand at the wrist, but he was able to maintain consciousness, despite the severe pain. Mark's workmates finally determined that there were two options available to free his hand from the conveyor belt. The first option was to manually remove the rollers of the conveyor belt so that Mark's hand could be released. This process would take a fairly long time. The second option was to reverse the motor of the conveyor belt. Doing so would allow Mark's hand to be backed out from between the rollers. This option would be quicker but would be much more painful. Both options were presented to Mark and he asked the workers to reverse the motor. He knew that waiting longer might cause him to lose consciousness and he was afraid of breaking his wrist. The employees reversed the wires and the rollers reversed direction, releasing Mark's hand from the machinery.

Mark was seen within the medical department of the assembly plant and they determined that there weren't any broken bones, so he decided to continue working through the night. When Mark got home I saw his hand for the first time. It was black and blue and resembled a large claw. Due to the large amount of swelling in the hand, it was difficult to see his fingers. His hand looked horrible.

The next morning Mark decided to see a specialist. We waited for several hours in the waiting room without being seen, and Mark was in terrible pain. We had grown so tired of waiting that we almost left the office. On our way out the door, however, the doctor met Mark. He took one look at Mark's hand and told him that he needed to be admitted to the hospital right away. He was afraid that Mark might have blood clots that could break free and possibly kill him. Once Mark was admitted to the hospital his hand was elevated and packed in ice. The medical staff examined the hand and determined that there weren't any broken bones, but that there was extensive soft tissue damage. The doctors feared they would need to perform skin graft surgery.

Mark and I had a friend who used to ride a motorcycle. Our friend had been involved in a serious motorcycle accident and had required skin grafts over a good portion of his body.

Mark and I were well aware of the consequences of skin grafts. Our friend had always experienced problems with his grafts. They were always cracking and bleeding, especially in colder weather. They also left ugly scars. I didn't want to see Mark have skin grafts, so I began to pray.

I always had a quiet corner in the house where I prayed. Mark's mother Stella had told me how the old-time Nazarenes used to pray. They used to get down on their knees and pray until they were sure they had an answer from God. I was still a fairly new Christian, but I figured if this worked for them in the past that I was going to try it. I got down on my knees and I prayed for hours. I asked God to heal Mark's hand, so that he wouldn't require skin graft surgery. I told God that it was okay and I would understand if he decided not to heal Mark's hand completely, but that I had to have an answer and wasn't going to get up from my knees until I had his answer. After several hours of prayer I received my answer. An awesome feeling came over me and a small voice said that Mark's hand would be fine. I called Mark that night at the hospital and told him that his hand would be fine and that he wasn't going to require skin grafts.

The next morning Mark was scheduled for the skin graft surgery. I showed up at the hospital and there were many of Mark's friends there. I told them about my prayers and the answer that Jesus had provided me. Mark's friends didn't believe me. They laughed at me. One of Mark's friends even mocked me saying he had talked to God also, and that God had told him that Mark was going to need skin grafts. I was undaunted though and remained 100 percent sure that Mark wasn't going to require the skin grafts.

The doctors had Mark brought down to the surgical suite and began to clean his hand to prepare it for surgery. To their amazement the skin tissue was regenerating on its own! He informed Mark that he would need to remain in the hospital for quite some time but that it didn't appear that skin grafts would be required! Mark spent about seventeen days in the hospital with his hand immobilized in an elevated sling. His hand was iced continuously throughout the hospital stay.

If you were to look at Mark's hand today you would never know that it had been crushed. He has full use of both of his hands and his left hand shows no sign of the injury. In addition, Mark has very little pain in his left hand. He has much more arthritic pain in his right hand than he does in his left. I believe that when Jesus healed Mark's left hand he made it better than it ever was. I believe that Jesus cured everything that had ever been wrong with Mark's left hand. Once again, God showed what a caring and loving God he is. God's answer to prayer was, again, miraculous, timely, and awesome.

I found out later that there was a safety mechanism on this conveyor belt that had failed.

The safety mechanism was designed to expand and pop the second roller out if an object got caught in the conveyor belt. The failure of this safety mechanism allowed Mark's hand to be crushed. When the employees were determining their options for freeing Mark's hand, they mysteriously overlooked one of the most obvious options. There was a button designed to release the conveyor belt in this type of incident. None of Mark's coworkers were aware of this option. I learned that there had been two other similar incidents with this exact same conveyor belt system. OSHA reports were filed regarding these incidents. In the other two incidents, the safety button release mechanism had been attempted and failed. In both incidents the safety release mechanism actually caused a piece of the conveyor belt system to drop down, severing each employee's hand. In Mark's case his fellow employees mysteriously failed to realize that this option was available to them. I believe that God was looking after Mark. He allowed Mark to remain conscious, and then provided him the answer that would free his hand from the machinery and cause him the least amount of damage.

Mathew 4:23-25 says the following:

> *Jesus went throughout Galilee, teaching in their synagogues, preaching the good news of the kingdom, and healing every disease and sickness among the people. News about him spread all over Syria, and people brought to him all who were ill with various diseases, those suffering severe pain, the demon-possessed, the epileptics and the paralytics, and he healed them. Large crowds from Galilee, the Decapolis, Jerusalem, Judea, and the region across the Jordan followed him.*

This verse meant a lot to me as I was praying for Mark's hand to be healed. There is no doubt in my mind that Mark was protected by the Holy spirit when he got his hand caught between the rollers of that conveyor belt, and there is no doubt in my mind that Mark's hand was healed through prayer.

THE HEALING
o f MY HANDS

Soon after the twins were born, I started having severe problems with my hands. I had open sores on them and, at times, I could see all the way to the bones in my fingers. I also had such severe arthritis in my thumbs that it became very difficult for me to open or close my hands. I had been diagnosed with a severe case of eczema and arthritis. The combination of eczema and arthritis made it virtually impossible for me to accomplish many tasks with my hands. My hands were also extremely ugly and were becoming increasingly nonfunctional. I was embarrassed by their appearance and felt they were becoming more and more useless.

I had seen several specialists. They had tried several forms of treatment but nothing seemed to work. Furthermore, I found it difficult to perform any chores in the house on my own. Not only did I have eczema, I was also allergic to rubber gloves. I couldn't bear to have my hands in hot water or chemicals, so I had to put my hands in a normal pair of gloves and then wore a pair of rubber gloves over the normal gloves whenever I used hot water or chemicals. It was horrible. This meant that I often required Mark's help to clean the house or perform any chores. I even had a difficult time diapering the twins. Babies can be so wiggly and the diapers that we used didn't have tape to close them. We used safety pins. You can imagine how difficult it would be for someone with severe arthritis and eczema in her hands to operate a safety pin while the baby is wiggling all over the place.

I could barely work the safety pins and maintain control of a baby. My hands were so painful from the open sores that I found it very painful to do anything at all. This had become a real problem and I honestly didn't know what to do about it. It was a nightmare.

I became even more discouraged one morning when I visited our family physician. He looked at my hands and asked me if I had been spending a lot of money on them. I replied that I had been spending quite a bit of money on them and had seen several specialists. He told me that both of my ailments were incurable and that spending money was a waste of my resources and time. I felt that he wasn't giving me any hope of ever improving this situation. My hands were becoming more and more crippled, and I seemingly had no hope.

I was attending church on a regular basis, and it was at one of these services that a scripture really struck me.

James 5:14-15 says the following:

> *Is any one of you sick? He should call the elders of the church to pray over him and anoint him with oil in the name of the Lord. And the prayer offered in faith will make the sick person well; the Lord will raise him up. If he sinned, he will be forgiven.*

This scripture really meant a lot to me regarding the healing of my hands. When the pastor had completed reading this scripture, a lady in the congregation stood up to give her testimony. She said someone she knew had a malignant growth and was going to have surgery to have the growth removed. She indicated that the church had been praying for this person to be healed of the cancerous growth, and that the elders of the church had laid hands on her and had anointed her in the name of Jesus. The surgery had been scheduled to remove the malignant growth. Doctors had completed their final examinations prior to the surgery. They checked all of the X-rays a second time to be certain of what they would be dealing with when they operated on her.

The cancerous growth appeared on the X-rays, and there was little doubt that it was malignant. The tumor had grown to become quite large. The lady showed up on her day of surgery and was prepped. They placed her on the operating table and began the operation. When they opened her up to remove the cancerous growth, however, there were no signs of the cancerous growth anywhere in her body! She had been miraculously healed, and there was nothing for them to remove from her body. Of course, none of the doctors had any explanation to offer to her family. To them it seemed utterly impossible that the growth would have gone away completely on its own without surgery. There really is only one explanation for this. The lady was healed through Jesus and the prayers of the elders of the church.

After attending this service, I went home and talked to Mark. I told Mark that I, too, would like to be healed. I told him about the service that I had attended and told him that I believed Jesus had the power to heal my hands. I asked Mark how I might go about asking God to heal my hands. Mark told me to just pray to Jesus about my hands and ask him to heal them. Mark told me to pray to Jesus as if I were talking to a friend. That night I prayed. I told Jesus that I didn't think that my request was selfish, because I really did need my hands to take care of my family, yet they had become almost completely useless. I really did feel embarrassed to have anyone see my hands, because they looked so ugly. I told Jesus that I really needed my hands to take care of Mark and the twins, and I asked him to heal them.

The next morning, when I woke up, my open sores were completely healed! I couldn't see the bones or any of the open wounds on my hands. Not only that, but I found that I had no problem opening or closing them. My arthritis had been completely healed as well. This was truly a gift from God. I think it is so important that we form a relationship with Jesus. He really does love us, and he looks after us. He wants to nurture a relationship with us. He takes really good care of our lives. He watches how we're walking and he really helps us when we need help. It's important that we learn these lessons.

The LADY
in the
NEXT BED

My conversion to Christianity and my dedication to serving Jesus brought me to a point where I was very actively involved in all sorts of charity work. I was working for an organization called Christians United Reaching Everyone (CURE). The organization was a non-denominational charitable organization that worked in the inner city of Cincinnati. It was a wonderful organization responsible for renovating old homes in the inner city that were going to be demolished. People gave the organization time and material in order to refurbish these old homes so that destitute people might have a place to live. Most of these homes were very large, so there were usually several people living in the refurbished homes. CURE used this opportunity to feed these people, provide them with a place to live, and witness to them about how Jesus had worked within their lives, and how he had died for their sins so that they might have a personal relationship with their heavenly Father.

Many of the people who needed these homes were proud people without a lot of opportunities. Many of them were Appalachians who didn't have much education. They found it extremely difficult to find jobs that paid much money, and many of them simply couldn't afford housing. When I originally started working for CURE, I asked the organization if it would be possible for me to work with the teenagers. The response to my request alarmed me. I was told that very few teenagers took advantage of this program. This was because many of the people who lived in the inner city were drug-dependent and needed to supplement their incomes. As a result, many of their parents had turned their own children into prostitutes before they had even become teenagers. I found this news both alarming and disheartening.

I was told that there weren't any real opportunities to witness and work with teenagers, but that there would be an opportunity to witness to younger people. I had been working as the teen youth leader for many years at my church. I really felt that my prior experience would help me witness to the teenagers in the inner city. Obviously, God had other plans for me, however, because that opportunity just didn't exist in the CURE program. I knew God had led me to work in this program, and I was willing to go wherever he was leading. I knew that God had a purpose for me in the CURE program, and I was anxious to serve in any way I could, so I decided not to get too discouraged and looked for other areas where I might be able to serve Jesus.

I really enjoyed working for this organization. The people I worked with were wonderful. I really enjoyed witnessing to the people and working with them. The work was very fulfilling; however, I was a little uneasy about walking the streets of the inner city. I can remember many instances when I felt uncomfortable walking in to work. I frighten easily and, at times, I found it difficult to avoid being completely terrified. I faced my fear, however, by praying for God's protection. I knew that as long as I was doing God's work he would protect me from anything I might encounter on the streets of Cincinnati.

One morning I parked my car and began to walk to work. I was feeling very ill on this particular morning and had been in a lot of pain. I had always lived with pain, however, because of my many female problems, and I really didn't think my pain was anything to be overly concerned about. I soon realized, however, that I needed to be concerned, because I kept getting sicker and sicker throughout my workday. I finally had to leave work and drive home. By the time I got home I was vomiting blood. I called the doctor and was immediately admitted to a hospital.

Apparently I had been hemorrhaging that morning as I walked into work, and had been bleeding internally for much of the day. Consequently, I had lost a lot of blood. Mark met me at the hospital and the doctors ran a lot of tests. The tests couldn't determine what was causing my bleeding. The doctors wanted to get my bleeding under control before they performed surgery, so they placed me on bed rest in order to limit my activity. Even though I was bedridden, they couldn't get my bleeding to stop.

I had been captive in bed for several days and had really gotten to know the woman in the bed next to mine. She was a very sweet lady. Her husband and mother had been to the hospital on several occasions, so I got to know them all quite well. They were all extremely nice people. Mark was working a lot of hours at the assembly plant, so they used to bring me food, because they knew the hospital food wasn't that great. They were really caring people, and I enjoyed visiting with them.

The lady was very ill. Her stomach was distended to the point that hospital caregivers had to drain water from her stomach on several occasions. At first the doctors didn't know what was wrong with the lady. They ran several tests on her and finally took her down to surgery for additional tests. When she returned from surgery, she received some very bad news. The tests revealed that she had cancer and that it had spread throughout her body. The doctors told her there was very little that could be done for her. She was told that the cancer was at such an advanced stage that it couldn't be treated effectively. The doctors told her they would do everything they could to make her as comfortable as possible, but said that she was dying and that nothing could be done to save her life.

The woman was very upset, as you can imagine. The news wasn't a great surprise to her, because she knew she was very ill, but she was upset that she was dying and there was very little hope for her. She told me that she was very frightened of dying. She told me that she had never really thought about death, but now she had come face-to-face with it, and it was a terrifying experience. She said that she had seen me praying a lot in my bed and that she was pretty sure that I was a Christian. I told her I was a Christian and I asked her about her background. She told me she was Catholic but she hadn't been going to church on a regular basis. She didn't know for sure that she was going to heaven when she passed away, so she asked if I could pray for her. I asked her if she had a personal relationship with Jesus. She told me that she had never really prayed directly to Jesus. When she prayed she often prayed to the saints, but never directly to Jesus.

I told her that I would pray for her, and I took the opportunity to witness to her. I told her about all that God had done in my life. I told her about how God had healed my hands and how he had cared for me. I asked her if she wanted to have a personal relationship with Jesus and if she wanted to be sure of her salvation. She told me that she wanted to be sure of her salvation and wanted a relationship with Jesus, so I took the opportunity to share the plan of salvation with her. I told her that we are all sinners by nature and all of us fall short of the glory of God. I told her that God sent Jesus to die for our sins so that we might have a relationship with God. I told her that the only way we can enter into God's presence is to be blameless and free from sin. This is only attainable through the blood of Jesus. We prayed together that night, and I have no doubt that she received her salvation. I continued to comfort the lady for as long as I was in the hospital. I really felt truly blessed to have been placed in the same room as this lady, and I was happy to do whatever I could to help comfort her in the hospital.

I think it's important that we, as Christians, give some outward signs of our faith in Jesus. I had the opportunity to witness with her, because she had seen me praying in my hospital bed. She sensed that I was a Christian, and this provided the opportunity for her to approach me about my beliefs. Had I not been showing my beliefs in an outward manner I'm not sure I ever would have had this incredibly important conversation with her. The more open we are with our beliefs the more opportunities we will have for people to approach us. This provides a great opportunity for witnessing to others. We also need to be aware of the fact that we can have a very personal relationship with our God through Jesus.

The Bible makes it clear that Jesus died on the cross for our sins so that we might have a personal relationship with our heavenly father. The Bible teaches us that we should pray directly to Jesus. Jesus will hear our prayers and present them to our heavenly Father. He died on the cross so that he could talk directly to God on our behalf. In 1 John 2:1 it says, "My dear children, I write this to you so that you will not sin. But if anybody does sin, we have one who speaks to the Father in our defense — Jesus Christ, the Righteous One."

And in 1 Timothy 2:5, it says, "For there is one God and one mediator between God and men, the man Christ Jesus."

The doctors wanted to get the bleeding stopped prior to taking me down for surgery, but they were unable to. I had lost so much blood that I was becoming anemic. The doctors decided not to wait any longer, and took me down for surgery. The surgery went well, and I was wheeled back to my hospital room. I was recovering from heavy medication and really felt woozy, but I continued to talk with the lady in the next bed, and tried to comfort her as best I could. At one point during the night the nurses came into the room and helped place the lady on a bedpan so that she could relieve herself. After awhile I noticed that the lady was crying. I asked her what was wrong, and she told me that she had been ringing for the nurses for a long time, but none came to help her off of the bedpan. She felt that the nurses had forgotten her. I tried ringing the nurses as well but none responded to my call either. This floor of the hospital was very busy and I'm sure the nurses were very busy as well. I, however, knew that the lady was in a very uncomfortable position and I wanted to do something for her.

Despite the fact that I had been told not to get out of bed, I felt I had to do something, so I got out of bed and started to walk down the hall to the nurses' station. I was holding onto the wall because I was still very dizzy from all of the medication. It took me quite a while to stumble down the hall to the nurses' station, but when I got there I told the nurses that the lady needed help getting herself off of the bedpan. The nurses met me rudely. They scolded me for being out of my bed and told me that they had heard our calls but were very busy and were unable to help us. They told me that someone would be in to help the lady shortly. In fact, one of the nurses escorted me back down the hall and made sure I made it back to my bed safely. The nurse then helped the lady off of her bedpan.

I was happy that I was able to help the lady and was happy that the nurse had taken her off of the bedpan. I can just imagine how uncomfortable that must have been for her, and she had already been through enough. The nurse, however, wasn't through with me. After she had helped the lady she came back to my bed and scolded me again for walking down the hall on my own. She informed me that she was the nurse who was responsible for everyone on this floor, that she had heard our calls and would have responded to them.

She said that she had been incredibly busy, but would have eventually answered our call for help. She told me that I was on too much medication to be walking the halls of the hospital. She said if I had fallen and hurt myself it would have been a liability issue and she would have been in a lot of trouble. Furthermore, she took the opportunity to tell me that I shouldn't have even been placed on this floor of the hospital, which was for critically ill patients. Everyone else on this floor had very severe illnesses, and most of them had no hope of ever being cured. She told me that I only had female problems and she was very upset that she had to care for me as well as all of the other critically ill patients on her floor.

I'm always interested to find out how God works. I knew that there was a reason that I was placed in this particular room of the hospital. I told the nurse I had no part in the decision to place me in this hospital room. I asked her if there were enough rooms available on the other floors of the hospital where she felt I should have been placed on the day of my admission. I wanted to know under what circumstances the hospital had decided to place me in this room. The nurse told me that she was very upset that I had been placed on this floor of the hospital and that she had checked into the availability of rooms on the floor where I should have been placed. She said that there were plenty of rooms available on that floor of the hospital the day I was admitted. She said she had no idea why I had been placed on this floor and that it was an unnecessary burden on her.

There seemed to be absolutely no reason why I should have ever been placed in this hospital room. Not only that, but my placement in this room was causing a lot of problems for this particular nurse and she had been trying to get me moved to another, more appropriate room the entire time I had been staying in the hospital. For whatever reason, she was never successful in her attempts to get me moved to a different room. I have no doubt that God placed me in this hospital room.

God made sure I was placed in this room and made sure I wasn't moved out of this room. There was a need for me to witness to the woman who was critically ill in the bed next to mine and God made sure I had the opportunity to witness to her and comfort her in her time of need. God works in mysterious ways. He truly is a caring and loving God.

Acts 1:8 says, "But you will receive power when the Holy Spirit comes on you; and you will be my witnesses in Jerusalem, and in all Judea and Samaria, and to the ends of the earth."

This verse tells us that Christians are given power to witness for the Holy Spirit. The verse tells us that we will receive power from the Holy Spirit and that we will witness for him to the ends of the earth. The Holy Spirit placed me in this situation to witness to a lady who was in need. She needed to be comforted and assured that she was going to heaven when she died. The Holy Spirit was responsible for setting up the unusual circumstances by which I was admitted to this hospital room. I had no part in the selection of my hospital room. Furthermore, there were valid reasons why I should have never been admitted to this hospital room. There really is only one explanation. The Holy Spirit felt it was important that this lady was comforted in her time of need, so that she might die with the assurance that God loved her and that she had received her salvation through his mercy.

That same night the woman went into cardiac arrest. Several nurses and doctors rushed into the room and they were able to resuscitate her. The woman and I were both discharged from the hospital, but I had grown so close to her that I continued to keep in contact with her after we left the hospital. It wasn't long, however, before she died. I thanked God that I had been given the opportunity to witness to her and comfort her in her time of need. As a result of my witnessing to this woman, I believe her husband and possibly even her mother came to know Jesus as their personal savior. I'm sure that when the woman died she went to heaven. God places his witnesses exactly where they need to be. He put me in that hospital room to witness to a frightened lady who didn't have a personal relationship with her heavenly Father.

God will sometimes put you in the strangest places to serve as his witness. The awesome thing is that God placed me exactly where I needed to be. I should have never been placed in that room of the hospital. In fact, I should have never even been placed on that floor of the hospital. I should have never crossed paths with the lady who was dying of cancer. God, however, made sure I was placed where I needed to be in order to do his work.

FLOWERS
for the
PASTOR'S WIFE

I had been very active as the youth leader for the teens at the church that Mark and I considered to be our home church for quite a few years. I had grown to dearly love the church but, for various reasons, Mark and I felt we needed to leave the church for a period of time. While attending other churches, however, we always kept tabs on our home church. One day, when I was working as the youth director of a different church, I had an unmistakable calling from the Holy Spirit that I needed to return to my home church. Obedient to God's call, Mark and I attended a service the next Sunday at our home church. During that service the pastor announced that he felt called to leave our home church because God was leading his life in a different direction. His announcement surprised Mark and me, and we both felt that there was a reason God had led us back to our home church. We didn't know if it had anything to do with the pastor's announcement but God's leading was unmistakable, and I felt I needed to be obedient, so Mark and I remained at our home church.

Both Mark and I were happy to be back in our home church. I wasn't actively serving in the church, but I was attending the services on a regular basis. At this time in my life I wasn't working outside of the home. I really wanted to spend all the time I possibly could with Tami and Tom before they started attending school on a full-time basis. Mark and I made the decision that we were going to live on a single income.

We had to watch our money a bit, but we always seemed to have enough. We tithed regularly, and I watched as God provided for all of our needs. Money was always tight, but we always had enough to do whatever we wanted.

One morning as I was driving my car, I suddenly sensed the Holy Spirit directing me to buy a bouquet of flowers and take them to the pastor's wife. I started to argue with God in my mind. I told him that I thought this request was crazy. I told him that I barely knew the pastor or his wife, and I couldn't just go to their house with a bouquet of flowers. I told him they would think I was crazy. I also told him that I didn't have any money to buy the flowers. I didn't have a credit card, so it wasn't like I could just charge the bouquet of flowers. This arguing went on back and forth in my mind for quite some time. Finally, I drove past a florist and I told God, "Fine, I'll go into that florist shop and I will buy whatever bouquet of flowers I can buy with the money I have in my wallet." I didn't have that much money, and I remember thinking to myself as I entered the florist shop that this was crazy. I told the Lord that I wasn't going to be able to buy flowers with the amount of money I had in my wallet.

As I entered the shop, however, I noticed that the florist was having a sale on daisies. I found that I had exactly the correct amount of money in my wallet to purchase a bouquet of daisies (down to the penny). I purchased the bouquet of daisies and left the florist shop. While I was on my way to the pastor's house, I continued to argue with God in my mind. I kept telling myself that this was crazy. I kept telling myself that I didn't even know these people and that this was going to seem crazy to them.

THE HAND of the HOLY SPIRIT

By the time I got to the pastor's house I had been arguing back and forth in my mind for quite some time. I walked up to the pastor's door and knocked. The pastor answered and I told him he didn't know me, but I attended his services on a regular basis. I told him I had purchased a bouquet of flowers for his wife. I told him this was going to sound crazy but I felt I had been led by God to buy these flowers and give them to his wife.

The pastor looked at me and told me I needed to give the flowers to his wife. He told me this was very important. I found the pastor's wife in the study of their home. When I gave the flowers to his wife she started to cry. She was crying quite a bit, so I thought I had done something wrong. I started to apologize to her for bringing the flowers to her. She stopped me from apologizing and told me that she had been praying for wisdom from God. She told me they felt God was leading them in a different direction in their lives. She said she wanted to be sure she was doing the right thing, so she had asked for wisdom. She asked God for an unmistakable sign from him so that she would know what they were supposed to do. She told me she had asked God to provide a bouquet of daisies as a sign that he was leading their lives in a different direction!

James 1:5-8 says the following:

> *If any of you lacks wisdom, he should ask God, who gives generously to all without finding fault, and it will be given to him. But when he asks, he must believe and not doubt, because he who doubts is like a wave of the sea, blown and tossed by the wind. That man should not think he will receive anything from the Lord; He is a double-minded man, unstable in all he does.*

The Bible scripture makes it clear that we, as Christians, have a right to ask for wisdom from our heavenly Father. He has told us that he will grant wisdom to his followers, but that we must have complete faith in the Lord. We cannot doubt that he will provide wisdom when we ask for it. In this case, the pastor's wife had asked for wisdom from the Lord, and the Lord had answered her in an unmistakable manner.

I think it is truly amazing that I was fortunate enough to carry God's message to the pastor's wife. I was fortunate enough to be the bearer of daisies, and I was truly blessed by this experience. I had been arguing about doing this task the entire time I was performing it. It wasn't until I had completely performed the task for God that I realized why he had asked me to do this. It's important that we are obedient to God's calling. If we feel unmistakable that God is leading us in a direction, no matter how trivial it might be, we need to follow his calling.

It would have been very easy to say that this was just a crazy thought that had entered my mind. I could have very easily ignored this thought and gone on with the normal course of my day. I was obedient to the calling, however, and was truly blessed by this experience.

MY FATHER'S DEATH

My father moved away from Cincinnati and was living in New Jersey. My father was a very confused man for many years. He was bound by a fear of interacting with others to the point that oftentimes he couldn't leave the front porch of his home. He would sit on his porch and cry. He had become so paranoid that he had an extremely difficult time coping with the world.

One morning I received a telephone call from my father. I don't really recall the conversation but what I do remember is that my father sounded as if he had a terrible cold. I told him to make sure he took care of himself. Later that same day I received a second call from my father. This time he sounded much worse over the phone. I told him that he should see a doctor because he didn't sound well at all. That same night I received a third phone call.

I was told that my father had been admitted to the hospital and had been diagnosed with a severe case of pneumonia. The doctor had indicated that he probably wouldn't live through the night. I was determined to try to make the trip from Cincinnati so that I could say good-bye to my father before he passed away. I talked to my father's doctor and he indicated that even if I tried to make the trip from Cincinnati, he didn't think there was any chance that I would make it there before my father passed away. He thought it would be senseless to attempt the trip. At that point, I told the doctor that I was going to try to make the trip anyway. I didn't want my father to pass away before I had a chance to talk to him one last time.

I quickly contacted my sisters and we organized the trip to New Jersey. Several of us decided to make the trip, including Paula, Jackie, Aunt Suzie, Debbie, and me. We all loved Dad and wanted the chance to see him one last time. None of us had any money at the time, and we decided to make the trip in Paula's car. She had the best car (it was fairly new) and we knew it was important not to run into any automotive problems. It took a bit of time to organize everything, despite the feverish pace and frantic nature in which everyone in the family was operating. By the time we actually left Cincinnati it was well after 9:00 p.m. I wondered if we would still have a chance to see dad before he passed away.

Paula took the first driving shift, since it was her car. We had all decided to drive through the night and take turns at the wheel so that we always had someone "fresh" driving the car. The only stops we were going to make were for gas, food, and the occasional necessary restroom break. While we were on the way down I had the feeling that we should all pray together. I remembered in the Bible that God promised that whenever there are two or more gathered in his name that there he would be also. I knew that some of the people in the car weren't Christians but I told everyone that the Bible said that God would listen to our prayers. I asked everyone to please close their eyes so that we could say a short prayer, everyone except Paula, since she was driving.

I asked Paula to pray along with us with her eyes open and on the road. We prayed for two things that night in the car.

We prayed that we would all be given a chance to speak with my father before he passed away and that God would provide us safe passage through the night. When we had finished praying I remember noticing the time. In situations like this I'm always quick to look for the awesomeness of God. Whenever I say a prayer asking for something specific from God I always try to notice the time. I have found that God listens to our prayers and many times provides an immediate answer to them. Many times I have been genuinely blessed by paying attention to things such as this. I would find out later that this was, once again, one of those times.

A few hours into the trip we were traveling down the Pennsylvania Turnpike. The turnpike was a lonely stretch of road with very few stops along the way. At times it seemed we were on the road for hours without coming across an area where we could pull over, fill the car up with gas, or get something to eat. The situation seemed even lonelier since we were traveling through the night. It seemed, at times, that ours was the only car on the road.

Paula was getting tired and we came across an exit that had a gas station. We decided to pull over so that we could fill the car up with gas, get a few snacks, and change drivers. While we were filling the car up with gas, Paula fell asleep in the back seat of the car. She was exhausted from driving so many hours.

After we gassed up the car and bought a few snacks, we decided that I would drive the rest of the way into New Jersey. I turned the key in order to start the car but the car wouldn't start. I thought maybe I wasn't starting the car right since this was such a new automobile. I had never been in a car like this before. Debbie was in the front seat of the car so we decided to pull the owner's manual out of the glove box and read through it to make sure there wasn't some "special procedure" that we had to go through in order to start the car. Paula was so exhausted that we didn't want to wake her. As we were fumbling through the owner's manual Paula woke up on her own.

She thought it was pretty funny that Debbie and I were reading through the owner's manual to figure out how to start her car. She also tried to start the car but she couldn't start it either. Now we found ourselves sitting in a gas station somewhere along the Pennsylvania Turnpike in the early hours of the morning with a car that wouldn't start. We had tried to avoid any automotive problems, but it seemed we had encountered the very thing we were most worried about. We knew if we had any serious problems with the car we would never finish the trip in time to see my father before he passed away. This situation really concerned all of us because none of us knew the first thing about cars, so we had no idea how to troubleshoot the problem.

We walked into the gas station and explained our situation to the attendant that night. We told him that our father was dying and that we had to make the drive to New Jersey before he passed away.

The gas station attendant wasted no time and decided to see if there was something he could do to help us. He looked under the hood of the car and found that every cell in the battery was completely dry. He said he had never seen anything like it in such a new automobile. He had a new battery and quickly swapped our battery with the new one so that we could continue our trip. He indicated that it was extremely lucky that we had decided to stop at his gas station. He said that there wasn't another stop for miles down the road. Had we not pulled into his gas station there was no way we could have made it to the next stop with a dead battery. We could have been stranded for hours. Since we were traveling through the night, there would have been very little traffic on the road, and we may not have received any help from another motorist until the next morning. This was well before the age of cellular phones, so there wasn't any way for us to get help had we become stranded. To be honest with you, I don't know how we made it as far as we did with a battery that was bone dry. The car lasted for as long as it needed to last and as soon as we found a safe place to pull over it failed.

I strongly believe that there is no such thing as "luck." I believe that God's hand is involved in everything and I have no doubt that his hand was at work once again in our lives. I believe the Holy Spirit made sure that Paula got tired and had to pull off the road at this particular exit. She got tired at the precise moment that led us to pull off at this gas station. Either that or God made sure that the car lasted long enough to get us to a safe place where we could swap out the battery and continue our trip. Either way, the hand of the Holy Spirit was definitely at work.

We made the rest of the drive without incident and arrived at the hospital in the morning. Miraculously, my father was still alive. I say it was miraculous for a very good reason. I talked to the doctor as soon as we arrived at the hospital and asked if we could see my father. The doctor said it was amazing that my father was still alive. He indicated that during the night (while we were on the road) my father had died. He said that another doctor just happened to be walking past my father's room that night at the precise moment that my father's monitors stopped registering his vital signs. The quick action of this doctor to resuscitate my father had saved his life that night. Had that doctor not been in the hall at precisely that instant my father would have most assuredly died. Something registered within me to prompt the doctor for the time of night that this occurred. The doctor indicated the time of night and I was awestruck — it was the exact time that I had the feeling that we should pray in the car. Once again, God's awesomeness was revealed to me!

We each had a chance to talk to my father before he passed away. One thing bothered me. My father recognized everyone who talked to him except for me. I had to be called into the room several times to talk to my father. As soon as I left the room he would ask one of my relatives if I had made the trip down to see him. He never remembered talking with me. I couldn't understand this, so I asked the doctor about it. The doctor's response was one of disbelief. He said that with the amount of medication in my father's system it was amazing that he was even conscious, let alone able to carry on conversations with his family members. I remember his words distinctly.

He said, "You're completely healthy and your father is very sick. Now, if I had given you the same amount of medication that I gave your father, you would be completely unconscious by now. I can't understand why your father can still carry on conversations. It doesn't surprise me at all that he can't remember having spoken to you. What surprises me is that he can carry on a conversation at all!"

Again I was awestruck. I remembered our prayer that night in the car. We had prayed for two things. One request was for safe travel. The other request was that each family member have a chance to speak to my father before he passed away. God had answered both of our prayer requests in a miraculous manner!

I had a difficult time with my father's death. I was very close to both my mother and father and his death really affected me to the point that, even today, I have some of his old possessions that I can't bear to look at. I was thankful to God that I had a chance to talk to my father before he passed away, even if he couldn't remember the conversations that we had that day in the hospital.

T h e
OUIJA BOARD

The use of the Ouija board started in the United States and Europe in the mid-nineteenth century. The first Ouija board patent was awarded in 1891. The original purpose was to seek contact with the spirits of the dead, and so the board gained popularity as the occultic Spiritualist movement gained momentum in the United States. The manufacturing company advertised it as a board game. Their slogan was, "It's just a game – isn't it?" However, even the advertisement campaign of a large toy manufacturer could not erase the evil purpose of the Ouija board. It was designed as a tool for the occult in the spiritualist movement as a means for seeking information and guidance from the spirits of the dead. The Bible makes it clear that we, as Christians, are to stay clear of witchcraft, sorcery, and other occult movements. Christians should never seek to use the Ouija board, even though it has been marketed as a harmless game board by Milton Bradley.

Deuteronomy 18:9-13 says the following:

> *When you enter the land the Lord your God is giving you, do not learn to imitate the detestable ways of the nations there. Let no one be found among you who sacrifices his son or daughter in the fire, who practices divination or sorcery, interprets omens, engages in witchcraft, or casts spells, or who is a medium or spiritist or who consults the dead. Anyone who does these things is*

detestable to the Lord, and because of these detestable practices the Lord your God will drive out those nations before you. You must be blameless before the Lord your God.

This scripture passage makes it clear that Christians are not to involve themselves with the occult or spiritualism. I, however, was never taught to stay away from the occult in the Methodist church that I attended in Cincinnati as a child. My church never talked about the occult or warned against getting involved with spiritualism. As a result, I had no idea that consulting the Ouija board was considered a sin. Nor did I realize the sordid history of the Ouija board and how it came into existence.

Paula, my sister, and I started using the Ouija board before I was married to Terry, my first husband. We didn't see anything wrong with using the Ouija board. We thought it was great entertainment and we were really surprised by the accuracy of some of the answers we got from the board. We seemed to be able to concentrate and work the board really well to gain answers to our questions. Paula always believed that we had some sort of gift of prophecy and that the Ouija board helped us tap into that gift.

Paula and I used the Ouija board quite often when I was married to Terry. Terry had mental problems. He was diagnosed with schizophrenia soon after we were married. He could become very violent at a moment's notice, causing a lot of problems in our relationship. I seemed to spend every other weekend at my mother's house. In fact, I got to the point where I could be packed and out of the house very quickly.

It seemed I could never really relax with Terry because of his violent nature. While I was experiencing these marital problems I often consulted the Ouija board for answers.

Paula and I used to try to find out all sorts of answers about our relationships. For instance, one time I asked the Ouija board if I would ever have children. I had always wondered about this because I had such terrible female problems and had been told that it was impossible for me to have children. The Ouija board indicated that I would have two children. Not only that, but it indicated that I would become pregnant only once, and that Terry would not be the father of my children. The Ouija board had predicted the birth of my twins long before I ever became pregnant with them. I've never been able to understand how or why the Ouija board worked for Paula and me. I don't know if it had something to do with the board itself or if it had something to do with contacting the spiritual realm. Paula and I, however, always received fairly accurate results from the Ouija board, and this bolstered our belief in the use of the board. It also bolstered Paula's belief that we had a gift for prophecy.

My relationship with Terry was getting steadily worse, and I finally had to file for divorce. I divorced and remained single until Terry's death. After his death in an automobile accident, I started dating Mark. Mark's father had been a Nazarene pastor. His father and mother had a very active ministry while his father was still alive, and Mark's mother had told him many stories about things they encountered during their ministry.

Mark's mother had always warned Mark to stay away from anything that had to do with an idol, the occult, sorcery, or witchcraft. She had seen some pretty strange things during the early years of their ministry, and she firmly believed that Christians had no business having anything to do with the occult. Mark's mother could tell stories that would make your hair stand up about encounters with demons and evil spirits. It was difficult for me to believe her stories, even though I knew they were from a credible source. I knew evil spirits and demons existed, but I never really gave them that much thought.

Mark let me know on many occasions that he felt my use of the Ouija board was appalling. He felt that any answers that came from the Ouija board were from demons and were evil by their very nature. Neither one of us was a very strong Christian at this time, but Mark knew it was not a good idea to get involved with anything that was related to the occult.

Despite his numerous warnings I didn't think there was anything wrong with using the Ouija board. I thought it was just an entertaining way for Paula and me to get answers to our questions. So I continued to consult the Ouija board even after Mark and I were married. One night while Mark was working nights at General Motors, Paula and my mother came over. I knew he wasn't going to be home until very early the next morning, so I used the opportunity to consult the Ouija board. Paula had just gotten a divorce from her husband, and was getting pretty serious about a man she had started dating. She wanted to know if her current relationship with this man was going to lead to anything.

What she really wanted to know is whether or not the man would ever ask her to marry him. We had decided to consult the Ouija board about this. My mother was sitting on a chair while Paula and I worked the board. While we were asking questions of the Ouija board some really crazy things started happening. Neither Paula nor I had ever seen the board act the way it did that night.

The board started spelling out, "Stop. This is not permitted." Paula and I were concentrating so that we could find the answer to our question, but the board continued to act strangely. It kept spelling out, "Stop. This is not permitted." Then it started to spell out, "Pam, Paula, don't stop — concentrate. I must get through." Neither Paula nor I knew what was going on. We seemed to be getting conflicting answers from the Ouija board. Something crazy was happening though because the Ouija board puck was going crazy. It was moving all over the board. The conflict seemed to go on for quite some time. While all of this was going on with the board, the room started to get colder and colder. It was as if there was an evil presence in the room. It made my mother so uncomfortable that she asked Paula and me to stop. She said she was freezing and that something strange was going on. She wanted no more of the Ouija board that night. I was getting a little nervous as well. After all, Mark had been telling me how evil the Ouija board was and how wrong it was to use it. I had never paid much attention to his warnings before, but now I was really getting nervous.

Though my mother and I were a bit afraid and nervous, Paula and I were determined to keep using the Ouija board.

We really wanted to know if Paula was going to marry the man that she had been seeing. Besides, the board kept spelling out that we shouldn't stop. It told us to concentrate harder. It kept telling us that someone or something was trying to break through. Then, all of a sudden, the Ouija board spelled out, "Pam, Paula, this is your father. Stay in church." My father had been dead for several months, so this was eerie. Right after we received the message "from my father," the board spelled out once again, "This is not permitted." As soon as it completed that last message, the puck shot across the room so hard that it hit the wall on the other side. It was as if it had been thrown, but neither Paula nor I had thrown it. I recognized that there was some other presence in control of that puck, and it scared me so much that I have never since consulted the Ouija board. I don't know how or why it works but I know enough to stay away from it. It has something to do with the occult. The Bible makes it clear that Christians should have no part of occult activities. This was a real learning experience for me.

When Mark got home from work, I told him what had happened, and we got rid of the Ouija board. I will never consult another Ouija board as long as I live. This story may sound pretty far-fetched, but it actually happened, and it scared me immensely.

MY FATHER'S RING

After my father died, I inherited a ring that he had always worn. The ring depicted Buddha with a diamond in his forehead and a snake wrapped around his body. When I accepted the ring, I realized that it represented an idol. I knew it was wrong for me to keep it, but I rationalized accepting the ring by recalling how cherished it was to my father. I never really felt comfortable having this ring but I couldn't bear to part with it. So I just left it in my jewelry box. Soon after I brought the ring home, however, strange things started happening, like strange noises that Mark and I had not previously heard in the house. These strange occurrences went on for quite some time.

One night, while Mark was still working nights for General Motors, I put the twins to bed and settled down with a good book. I was pretty engrossed in the book, but something caught my attention. I noticed what looked like the tails of a trench coat swiftly enter Tami and Tom's bedroom. Initially, I thought, "Oh, my God, I've been reading so intently that I didn't notice that someone has broken into the house and entered the twins' room." At this point I was extremely frightened, as I'm sure anyone would have been. I knew that I had to go into my children's room and confront whomever had broken into the house. I didn't have any weapons or anything that I could use to harm whoever was in that room, but I knew that I had to defend my children. When I got up from bed I said a short prayer to

Jesus. I told Jesus that I didn't have anything with which to protect myself but that I had to protect my children.

I asked for his protection, and I began walking toward my children's room.

As I took my first few steps toward my children's room, I suddenly had a feeling come over me that whatever was in that room was not a man. I knew unmistakably that whatever was in that room was an evil spirit. This realization stopped me dead in my tracks for a moment, but I remembered 1 John 4:4 (KJV) that states, "Ye are of God, little children, and have overcome them: because greater is he that is in you, than he that is in the world." I knew at that moment that I served a God that was much more powerful than anything I would encounter in that room. I said another quick prayer, asking God to protect my children and me. I then prayed in the power of the blood and in the name of Jesus Christ who died on the cross that the Lord would cast out whatever was in that room and protect my children from that evil spirit. As soon as I had completed my prayer a great deal of commotion broke out in my children's room. I heard toys hitting against the walls and the door of the room.

When I went into the room, the toys were laying scattered all over the floor of the room. Every night I had a habit of making sure that the entire room was picked up and neat before putting Tami and Tom down for the night. My children had always gone to bed in a clean room, and this night was no exception. Even more remarkable was the fact that neither Tami nor Tom woke up, even though all this commotion took place around them. This was incredibly strange and I was incredibly frightened. I was shaking from head to toe because I firmly believed I had encountered an evil spirit.

THE HAND *of the* HOLY SPIRIT

I thanked the Lord for his protection by saying another short prayer. As soon as I had stopped thanking him, however, I had another thought. The thought occurred to me that not everyone in our family was safe at home yet. Mark would have probably been on his way home from work at about this time. Having gone through this experience, I feared for his safety as well. I said another short prayer, telling the Lord that not everyone was present in my home, and asking for his protection for all members of my immediate family. I asked him to keep them safe from anything evil.

When Mark came home from work he noticed that something was unusual. As soon as he saw me he knew that something had happened. He said that my eyes were huge and that I looked like I had seen a ghost. At that, I asked Mark if anything strange had happened to him that night. He initially told me that he couldn't think of anything. I asked him again to think hard. I told him that something had happened at the house, and I wanted to know if anything strange had happened to him this night.

Mark said, "Come to think of it, something strange did happen to me on my way home from work tonight. I fell asleep behind the wheel of the car. My eyes opened just in time for me to realize that I was in the gravel of the shoulder of the road. I was able to get the car back on the road and I made it home just fine, though."

After Mark told me about this incident I told him about what had happened that night at the house. I hadn't picked up the toys in the children's bedroom yet and I showed them to him. He said he honestly believed what I had told him. His mother had told him all sorts of stories about her encounters with evil spirits during the early years of his father's ministry. He had no doubt that I had encountered an evil spirit this night. He asked me not to tell anyone, however, because he said that most people in the church would think I was crazy and they wouldn't believe me.

I honestly believe the evil spirit that was thrown out of the house went after Mark on his way home from work that night. I believe Mark would have been involved in a serious automobile accident had the Holy Spirit not protected him. That might seem to be the product of a highly imaginative mind but it seems pretty coincidental to me that I would have had the thought that not all members of my immediate family were present in my house at the moment the evil spirit was thrown out of the house. It's also pretty coincidental that Mark would have fallen asleep behind the wheel of his car on this same night and would wake up in time to get his car back on the road safely. I have no doubt in my mind that the Holy Spirit protected Mark from the evil spirit that had been in my house that night.

The next day we asked for advice from Mark's mother, knowing that she had dealt with this type of situation in the past. We asked her what we could do to protect ourselves from this. She told us to place some religious items in each of our bedrooms and throughout areas of the house. She said to place a picture of Jesus over our beds and to place an open Bible on our dressers. She said that we should also pray to Jesus for the protection of our house from the evil spirit. Mark and I did all of these things, but strange things just kept happening in our house. On one occasion a lady from church was visiting the house. I was the teen youth leader and she was one of my assistants.

While she was visiting, I placed Tami and Tom for a nap in their room. All of a sudden Tami started screaming bloody murder upstairs in her bedroom. We both went up to see what was going on. When I looked at Tami, her neck was red and bruised as if someone had tried to choke her. You could still see the imprints of thumb marks on her voice box. At first, I was about ready to beat the living daylights out of Tom, because I assumed that Tom had choked his sister. When I looked over at Tom, however, he was still asleep in his bed. My visiting friend told me that she felt something strange was going on in my house, and that I needed to talk with the pastor of our church.

I decided to take her advice and do exactly what Mark had told me not to do. When I talked to the pastor about the strange occurrences, he recommended that I not repeat the story to anyone else. He said that he didn't believe in evil spirits or demons. He said that evil spirits were things that were taught in the past but that the church no longer taught about or believed in the existence of evil spirits or demons. He believed that when the Bible was written, the only way people of that time knew how to describe mental illness was to say the person had been possessed by a demon, but he didn't actually believe in the existence of evil spirits. He thought I must have been imagining these things. This was the exact response that Mark had warned me about. I was extremely disappointed with his response. After all, if it makes sense to believe in angels doesn't it make sense to believe in evil spirits? The church readily talks about the existence of God's angels, but fails to talk about the existence of evil spirits. I believe one cannot exist without the other. I firmly believe what the Bible says, that demons and evil spirits are both in the world today. The Bible teaches us that when we become Christians we are engaged in spiritual warfare. It really shocked me that a pastor would say that he did not believe in evil spirits or demons.

1 John 4:1-4 says the following:

> *Dear friends, do not believe every spirit, but test the spirits to see whether they are from God,*

because many false prophets have gone out into the world. This is how you can recognize the Spirit of God: Every spirit that acknowledges that Jesus Christ has come in the flesh is from God. But every spirit that does not acknowledge Jesus is not from God. This is the Spirit of the antichrist, which you have heard is coming and even now is already in the world. You, dear children, are from God and have overcome them, because the one who is in you is greater than the one who is in the world.

This Bible verse clearly points out the existence of evil spirits. In addition, the Old Testament of the Bible is loaded with scriptures that talk about the existence of evil spirits. Throughout the New Testament Jesus is depicted as casting out demons. In one instance he casts out many demons from one man. The Bible says that the man had so many demons in him that they referred to themselves as "legion." Jesus cast the demons out of the man and allowed them to enter a herd of pigs. The pigs became startled and stampeded into the sea and were drowned. The Bible, in both the Old and New Testaments, attests to the existence of evil spirits. To doubt they exist is to doubt the validity of the Bible.

I knew some people in church whose parents were "old-time" Nazarenes who still held to the practices of the "old-time" Nazarenes. So I decided to talk to some of these people, since the pastor was of no help to me. I asked one of these women if she might have an idea about what was going on in my house. She came over to the house and prayed in each room. She didn't perform an exorcism, or anything like that, but she did pray for each of the rooms of the house. After she finished praying for the house, she asked me to make a list of everything that I brought into the house at about the same time these occurrences started. She told me that she had read stories that evil spirits could attach themselves to objects and that I may have brought an object into my house that had an evil spirit attached to it. Instantly I thought of my father's ring. I told her about the ring and she recommended that I have the ring destroyed.

I still couldn't bear to have the ring destroyed so I decided to place the ring in a jar and bury it in my backyard. I didn't want to take it to a dump because it was such a big part of my father's life. After I buried the ring in the backyard, there were several nights in a row that Mark and I heard noises outside the house. The noises were like cats fighting and squalling outside in the backyard and scratching on the glass patio door. Sometimes we would try to see what might have been going on, but we never saw anything. I was convinced that this had something to do with the ring that I had buried in the backyard.

I told my sisters about all of the incidents that seemed to surround this ring. I don't think either of them believed me because Paula told me that she wanted Dad's ring. I told Paula that I didn't want to give it to her, but she insisted that she really wanted it. She led me to believe that she was going to take it and have it destroyed, so I gave her the ring. At this time, Paula was happily married. She had a beautiful home, and she and her husband both worked for Ford Motor Company. They were doing quite well and seemed to have everything going for them. Within a few years of her receiving the ring, however, her marriage fell apart. She developed all sorts of physical problems and declared bankruptcy. I asked Paula if she still had Dad's ring, and she said yes! She never had it destroyed. I told her that I thought the ring was evil and that she should have it destroyed. I don't know if the ring had anything to do with what happened to Paula, but I really wanted her to destroy the ring. I still don't know if Paula ever destroyed it, but I really hope so because I have no doubt that an evil spirit or demon had attached itself to that ring.

TOM'S FIRST
DRIVING
LESSON

When the twins were a few years old, Mark's assembly plant was engaged in a "wildcat" strike. The strike was the result of Mark having thrown out the main UAW committeemen. The union then demanded that Mark be fired for this, but General Motors backed Mark completely. They transferred Mark to an assembly plant in Ypsilanti, Michigan, while negotiations proceeded for over six months.

During this time, I was having a wonderful time working as the youth leader of the teenagers at church. They were a lot of fun. Many came to know the Lord as personal savior and grew spiritually. One time I was picking up the teens to take them to the roller skating rink. I was running late, as usual. I pulled into the driveway of the apartment buildings where I was picking up two of the teens. I blew my horn, but they didn't come out. Because I was running late, I put the car in park, left Tami and Tom in the car with the motor still running, and went to check on the teenagers. I know it sounds irresponsible to leave young children unattended in a car but that was a long time ago, and times were different. Car seats and seat belts were not required and motor vehicles didn't have all of the standard safety features they now have. A feature to prevent putting the car in gear unless the brake pedal is engaged wasn't even thought of in those days.

This vehicle was a 1969 Chevrolet with a V8 engine, a four-barrel carburetor, and an automatic choke. The automatic choke was designed to idle the engine at around 1,500 – 3,000 RPMs when the engine was cold. Typically, in cold weather, it would take a while for the engine to warm up so the choke would remain engaged for quite some time. Once the engine warmed up, the gas pedal had to be pumped several times to disengage the choke. Well, just as I got out of the car to check on the teenagers Tom decided he wanted to drive. He took the car out of park and started down the driveway. That would have been bad enough, but to make things worse, this house was only about a half block from my house; the engine was still cold. I hadn't disengaged the choke because it was winter and the engine hadn't had a chance to warm up. The car was still idling at about 1,500 – 2,000 RPMs. When Tom took the car out of park, the car took off at a high rate of speed.

The driveway was long, steep, and narrow. At the end of the driveway was a parking lot with about fifteen to twenty cars parked, belonging to the residents of the apartment buildings. Along the left-hand side of the driveway was an apartment building. Along the right-hand side was a fieldstone wall that ran the entire length of the driveway. When Tom started down the driveway he was headed straight for the parked cars at the end of it. The car was going really fast. I started screaming and chasing the car. I don't know what I thought I was going to do — grab onto the back of the car and hold on? Maybe I was going to try to jump in and see if I could stop it? It was one of those moments where I felt completely helpless.

Every ounce of my soul wanted desperately to do anything to stop what I knew was about to happen, but I had no control over this situation and felt completely ill. While running after the car, I could see that it was going to crash into the cars that were parked at the end of the driveway. I knew that Tami and Tom weren't in their car seats, and I knew that a head-on collision at that speed would probably kill them. At that moment I started screaming to God. "God, help them! Do something! They're going to be killed, and I can't do anything! Help them!"

Suddenly, Tom steered the car to the right. The car struck the fieldstone wall, caving in the right side of the automobile. Hitting the fieldstone wall changed the direction of the car, sending it crashing into the apartment building that was on the left-hand side of the driveway. This crumpled the left side of the car as well but at least the car was no longer headed directly for the cars that were parked at the bottom of the driveway. Instead, it proceeded through an area at the front of the parking lot where no cars were parked, and headed straight for a chain link fence and a steep abutment. The abutment separated the apartment building from Interstate 75 — a major highway. The car ripped through the chain-link fence as if it was never there, destroying the front of the car. It ripped out the front grill, tore up the front end, and smashed the windshield.

From my perspective it didn't look like the chain link fence had any effect on the car's speed. The car started up the steep abutment and didn't seem to be slowing down at all! I had no doubt that it was going to roll right up onto Interstate 75 where it would be broadsided by oncoming traffic.

At this point I screamed like you couldn't imagine. I screamed to the Lord, "Help them, stop them, do something — Help me!" At that very moment, the car just stopped. It was as if the car had hit a large object that just stopped it, but it didn't jolt. The car just stopped. By the time it stopped, however, it had reached the top of the steep abutment. The front tires lifted off the ground, and the car started to flip backwards. I feared the car was going to flip end-over-end down the abutment. I cried, "God, do something, and do it now!" At that point it was as if a big hand from heaven came down and rested on the roof of the car. Very gently the front end came down and the car was on all four tires again. The car had ripped up the grass and mud on the way up the steep abutment. As a result, the car was unable to pick up any significant speed on the way back down the hill. It was as if a big hand slowly and gently pushed the car back down the hill and glided the car to a very soft stop at its bottom.

I practically flew down the driveway and got the twins out of the car. Somebody must have called the police, because they were on the scene now. The twins were shaken up quite a bit, but they were fine! When I got Tami out of the car, she looked at me and pointed her little finger at me, saying, "Daddy's going to kill you!"

I thought to myself, "Honey, you are so right."

I looked at Tom and I asked him, "What were you thinking?" Tom looked back at me and said, "I was thinking I was wishing my mommy was here!"

This incident took place in Arlington Heights near Cincinnati. This was a small community and everybody knew everyone else. The police officer that was at the bottom of the hill was a friend of mine.

He told me that he had clocked the car going 80 miles per hour at the bottom of the hill. He said he didn't know why, or how, Tami and Tom weren't severely injured or killed. The following Bible verses make it clear that God has ministering angels that care for the heirs of salvation. Furthermore, it appears that this ministering care begins in infancy and continues through life.

Hebrews 1:14: "Are not all angels ministering spirits sent to serve those who will inherit salvation?"

Matthew 18:10: "See that you do not look down on one of these little ones. For I tell you that their angels in heaven always see the face of my Father in heaven."

Psalms 91:11: "For he will command his angels concerning you to guard you in all your ways."

Psalms 34:7: "The angel of the LORD encamps around those who fear him, and he delivers them."

Daniel 6:22: "My God sent his angel, and he shut the mouths of the lions. They have not hurt me, because I was found innocent in his sight. Nor have I ever done any wrong before you, O king."

Matthew 2:13: "When they had gone, an angel of the Lord appeared to Joseph in a dream. 'Get up,' he said, 'take the child and his mother and escape to Egypt. Stay there until I tell you, for Herod is going to search for the child to kill him.'"

Matthew 2:19: "After Herod died, an angel of the Lord appeared in a dream to Joseph in Egypt."

Acts 5:19: "But during the night an angel of the Lord opened the doors of the jail and brought them out."

Acts 12:7-10: "[7]Suddenly an angel of the Lord appeared and a light shone in the cell. He struck Peter on the side and woke him up. 'Quick, get up!' he said, and the chains fell off Peter's wrists.'"

"[8]Then the angel said to him, 'Put on your clothes and sandals.' And Peter did so. 'Wrap your cloak around you and follow me,' the angel told him. [9]Peter followed him out of the prison, but he had no idea that what the angel was doing was really happening; he thought he was seeing a vision. [10] They passed the first and second guards and came to the iron gate leading to the city. It opened for them by itself, and they went through it. When they had walked the length of one street, suddenly the angel left him."

I thank God for keeping Tami and Tom safe through this incident. It was nothing short of a miracle that my car avoided hitting all of those cars parked at the bottom of the hill, and, while traveling at such a high rate of speed, failed to enter Interstate 75.

Either of these actions would no doubt have killed Tami and Tom. Likewise, even though they weren't in their car seats, they sustained no injuries, even though the car was a complete wreck.

A PICNIC at KINGS ISLAND

When I first became the teen youth leader at our church, I started with the junior high teens. After a period of time, however, our youth leader for the high school teens stepped down, so I ended up as the teen youth leader for both groups. I always had a wonderful time as the teen youth leader. I had a lot of teens who really grew in the Lord and I felt privileged that I had the opportunity to help them have a better relationship with the Holy Spirit.

I knew that if I was going to witness to these teenagers, I needed to get to know them better. Oftentimes we think we can just hand some stranger a pamphlet or talk to them about Jesus without getting to know them. Then, we wonder why they never come to church or trust in Jesus as their savior. I took the opportunity to get to know the teens better by having fun with them. In addition to studying God's word, many of the activities were designed to be fun and build fellowship within the group. This was an effective way to witness to the teens, because my group of teens knew that I absolutely loved them and cared about them. The two most important aspects of being a youth leader are getting to know the group that you are leading and to having fun with them.

While I was the youth leader I was involved in planning a trip to Kings Island, an amusement park near Cincinnati. At the time it was one of the largest amusement parks in the midwest.

The invitation to go was open to my teen group as well as teen groups from neighboring churches. There was also an open invitation to anyone who wasn't currently involved in a church.

I planned to give a short devotional with my teen group before leaving for Kings Island for a day of fun. While I was doing the devotional, however, one of my teenage girls came in wearing shorts. She was a somewhat rebellious teenager, and I sometimes had a difficult time with her. This wouldn't be a problem if it were to happen today, but at that time the Nazarene church didn't permit wearing shorts. They felt that wearing shorts exposed too much skin and that it was inappropriate. So, while we were waiting for her to change clothes, many more teens started showing up for the trip. I started looking at the amount of food we had and I thought, "Hmm, this could be a problem. I don't think there's enough food for all of these teens." Even more teens showed up, and I knew I didn't have enough food. The teens were supposed to have brought either box lunches or money to purchase food at Kings Island. Most of the teens didn't show up with box lunches, however, and I knew that most of them didn't have money to buy food. I was fairly sure that if they didn't come with a box lunch I was going to need to feed them.

We finally got everyone together and started piling into the cars. I had several helpers with me. We had planned on spending the entire day at Kings Island, having fun and riding the rides. Although I took potato salad, baked beans, and other picnic type foods, I didn't have an abundance of anything, and I knew I wasn't going to have enough.

One of my helpers also realized that not many teens had brought box lunches and knew that they had very little money. She asked me what we were going to do because we didn't have enough money to purchase food for all these teenagers — especially at an amusement park where everything was so expensive. I told her, "We have some food. I guess it will have to be enough." She replied, "I know Pam, but it isn't enough. What are we going to do?" I responded that it was just going to have to be enough food. We were just going to rely on the Lord to multiply the food as he did in the Bible. I told her that we were in a situation similar to that of the disciples when Jesus was speaking to the crowds of people, and there wasn't enough to feed them. I reminded her of how Jesus had multiplied the seven loaves of bread and few small fish in order to feed the thousands of people who had come to hear him speak. We would just rely upon Jesus to multiply the food.

After the teens had been enjoying the rides a long time, they came to us for lunch. I asked how many box lunches had been brought. There were very few, as we already knew. I told them that because we didn't have a lot of food with us, we were going to ask Jesus to bless and multiply it, as he had the loaves of bread and the fish in the Bible account. In my prayer I also acknowledged to the Lord that we didn't have much money and were going to be at Kings Island all day. I didn't want the teens to go hungry.

After I prayed we ate. As we were eating, I kind of laughed because the teens kept coming back for more and more food. The teens didn't seem to be holding back, but the food just didn't seem to be running out.

I told the woman helper that it really looked like the food was multiplying! The teens had plenty of food to eat and we even had food left over. In fact, the teens came back several times during the day to eat, and the food never ran out. There was enough food to feed the group of teens all day at Kings Island. This was another example of the Holy Spirit performing a miracle on our behalf.

Mark 8:1-13 says the following:

During those days another large crowd gathered. Since they had nothing to eat, Jesus called his disciples to him and said, "I have compassion for these people; they have already been with me three days and have nothing to eat. If I send them home hungry, they will collapse on the way, because some of them have come a long distance. His disciples answered, "But where in this remote place can anyone get enough bread to feed them?" "How many loaves do you have?" Jesus asked. "Seven," they replied. He told the crowd to sit down on the ground. When he had taken the seven loaves and given thanks, he broke them and gave them to his disciples to set before the people, and they did so. They had a few small fish as well; he gave thanks for them also and told the disciples to distribute them. The people ate and were satisfied. Afterward the disciples picked up seven basketfuls of broken pieces that were left over. About four thousand men were present.

In this Bible passage Jesus multiplied the food to feed the multitude of people that had come to listen to him. Likewise, we didn't have enough food to feed this group of teenagers. We prayed for God's blessing on the food and asked him to multiply it just as he had done in this scripture. By allowing God to bless and multiply the food we found we had plenty of food for the teenagers. We even had food left over, just as in this scripture.

Looking back on this incident, I think the worry that I had was kind of silly. After all, we probably could have gone all day without eating that much. I don't think it would have hurt any of us to be a little hungry but, at the time, it seemed like a really big problem. I can only thank the Lord that he understood this situation from my perspective and that he honored my prayer, even though most people would probably consider it a petty request. I think this incident points out the fact that Jesus listens to all of our prayers, no matter how petty they might seem in retrospect.

The FIRE on BLANCHE AVENUE

After my father's death my mother needed help keeping up with all of the rental properties that she and my father owned. Since Mark and I were the only ones who didn't own a home, we packed up all of our stuff and went to live with my mother on Blanche Avenue. We contacted our insurance representative when we decided to move into the house in order to figure out what we needed to do about our fire insurance policies. He informed us that we would need to cancel our insurance policy, because the house was in my mother's name and would be covered under hers. He said insurance companies would not pay on two policies for a single house in the event of a fire. Consequently, Mark and I cancelled our policy.

Mark and I lived with my mother for quite some time, but eventually we determined that we needed to obtain a place of our own. Mother was steadily recovering from the death of my father, and we determined that it was time for us all to move on with our lives. Mark and I decided that the best course of action was to move into an apartment close to Mother so that we could continue to help her with the rental properties, and provide a comfortable measure of distance for our family.

After a bit of searching we found a beautiful town house close to Mom's house. Although old, the house was well maintained and had spacious rooms with high ceilings. It suited our needs perfectly and Mark was ready to move in right away! Even though the house would be available on December 17, I convinced Mark to wait, and move into the house some time after the Christmas holiday season. I really wanted to spend the holidays with my mother, in her house, one last time.

In retrospect the decision to delay our move turned out to be a bad one. My mother's house caught fire on the night of December 17, the exact date that the town house would have become available. Had we decided to move into the town house that day all of our belongings would have been moved out of mother's house before the fire. This wasn't the case, however, and all of our material possessions were in the house when it caught fire. The fire was so severe that five fire trucks were dispatched. It even made the local news — both television and newspaper. Nearly all of our possessions were destroyed. Our only other major possession (our car) had been wrecked just weeks prior to the fire while parked on my aunt's street.

Mark and I had to start our lives over again. You know, I never really thought about how expensive it would be to replace all of the items lost in the fire. When you stop and think about all of the items in your own homes, the clothes, the toys, the furniture, and everything else, it really adds up to an astronomical sum of money. We had accumulated all of these possessions over the years, writing small checks for each item. When you accumulate items a little at a time you really lose sight of the total value of those items until you are faced with replacing them all at once. It was going to prove very difficult for us to start over from scratch. In addition to all of this, the reporters who documented the fire in the local newspapers and local televised news programs got all of the details wrong. They had inaccurate addresses and phone numbers for Mark and me, so if anyone wanted to send donations to help us through these difficult times, they would have a very difficult time tracking us down. I always felt it was a bit odd that all of our information was reported inaccurately. I oftentimes wonder if the hand of the Holy Spirit wasn't involved in this as well. What better way to show Mark and me that he would provide for all our needs than to isolate us from help from the news media and external means of support?

Through all of this Mark and I never felt an ounce of worry or discomfort. Mark and I were both young and Mark had a great job at General Motors. In addition, we had turned the matter over to God through prayer and we were sure that God would provide for our family. I can remember one instance specifically about the inner peace that I had throughout this entire ordeal. One morning after the fire I was walking down to a laundry facility in one of mother's apartment buildings. I was humming a church hymn, "He's able, He's able, I know my Lord is able …"

I was collecting the coins from the washing machines and thinking about the fire and how much we had lost. It occurred to me that Mark and I were really in a mess. Everything was going to be so expensive to replace. Mom was underinsured and we had canceled our home owner's policy. As a result, we didn't receive that much help from the insurance company. I wasn't really worrying about how we would replace it all, but I was thinking that we were in a pretty messy situation. Suddenly, an incredible feeling of inner peace came over me. A small voice told me not to worry, that everything was under control.

God did, in fact, have everything under control. God provided for all of our needs after the fire. The outpouring of love from everyone was truly remarkable. For instance, the day that Mark returned to work his boss met him at the door to tell him to go home and provide for his family. He told Mark that he had no business being at work when his family had no place to live and that he didn't want to see him back at the assembly plant until after the holidays were over and his family was settled. He assured Mark that he didn't have to worry about anything other than his family. His job would be taken care of. People from the assembly plant made sure that Mark and I attended the Christmas party where they presented us with a gift of about $2,500. Donations had poured in from people who worked with Mark. It was a unified effort of both hourly and salaried workers who empathized with our situation and wanted to do whatever they could to help us get back on our feet as quickly as possible. We were truly thankful for everything that we received and were deeply touched by the outpouring of love from everyone.

We received numerous donations of gifts, clothes, and other items from people we never knew. One of the amazing things was that most of the sizes and colors were perfect. Some clothing was older, but most everything we received fit perfectly. Other household items matched our furniture perfectly. The color and design were perfect. It was obvious to me that God was directing this entire effort, and was prompting people to provide all of the items we needed. I don't want to make it sound like absolutely everything was perfect. Some items we received were incorrect and a lot of stuff was old and sometimes not useful to our family, but there were unmistakable signs that God's hand was at work. This was a miracle coordinated by God. We received everything we needed through the numerous donations. God provided for all of our needs through the generous outpouring of gifts and donations.

It truly was amazing. I remember one incident specifically. One morning I walked over to the house of the fire chief of Cincinnati. The fire chief lived only a few doors down from us. As I said earlier, the newspapers and televised news reports didn't have any of our information correct, so most people didn't know where to send donations. As I was talking to the fire chief, a gentleman came to the house. He said he was a doctor, and that he had a donation for our family. The trunk of his car was filled with wrapped Christmas presents for our family. It bothered him that our children had lost all of their toys and clothes in the fire and he felt led to provide us with gifts for Christmas. As we talked I asked for his name. He said I didn't need to know his name, only that this was something he wanted to do for us. I am truly grateful to that gentleman for his outpouring of love during a difficult time in our lives. I believe he was led by the Holy Spirit because every gift that we received from him was perfect. All of the items of clothing fit each of us perfectly. There wasn't a single item that didn't fit or wasn't the right color. These were indeed gifts from God!

There was another incident that sticks out in my mind. After Mark and I moved into the town house, we continued to receive gifts and packages that were providing for our needs. I was truly grateful, but one night I was in the town house and I noticed that one wall had a fireplace that ran down the middle. There were two tall and narrow windows on either side of the fireplace. They weren't standard sized windows. I remember thinking; "Hmm, God, I wonder what I can do about those windows. We have so much other stuff to replace from the fire that I can't possibly afford to go out and buy custom drapes for these windows. What am I going to do about that?" I didn't share this thought with anyone.

One morning I went to our Bible Study class. As I was walking into the class one of my friends stopped me. She was carrying a package, a delivery from her mother to me. She said her mother had been praying one night, and she received a clear message from God that I could use these drapes. She said that she had been told, through prayer, that she should go up to her attic and find these drapes. Her mother found these drapes and had them dry cleaned for me. Not only were they beautiful, they were the perfect length for the two windows! I didn't even need to hem them. The colors were perfect for the room, taupe mixed with soft green and orange hues. To be honest with you I don't think I could have gone out and purchased a nicer pair of drapes for that room. It was amazing how God supplied all of our needs after the fire on Blanche Avenue. He truly does take care of his followers.

Philippians 4:19 (KJV) says, "But my God shall supply all your needs according to his riches in glory by Christ Jesus."

God truly did respond to all of our needs during this difficult time in our lives. He did it through the tremendous outpouring of love from other people. He made sure that every need was met.

This was a very difficult situation for us. Mark and I have always been extremely proud people. Mark especially hates to take gifts from others, and he felt very uncomfortable about receiving all the gifts and donations from everyone who showed genuine concern regarding our situation. Everyone was so generous. The outpouring of gifts and love was truly remarkable. Mark had a difficult time, because he never felt that he was destitute throughout this incident. He knew that he could recover from the fire on his own. He was young and had a good job. He had lost nearly everything, but there was plenty of time to recover from such a devastating fire. Looking back on this incident, I really think the Lord used this as a learning experience for both of us. I think he really wanted to show us that he was capable of providing for all of our needs. Up to this point in our lives Mark and I always felt really self-sufficient. Through this incident, however, we learned that we could rely upon the Lord for everything that we needed. We learned that the Lord is a wonderful provider for our needs and that we could rely upon him for anything.

A ROOM
UNTOUCHED
by FIRE

Mark's mother didn't have any income at the time of the Blanche Avenue fire. She didn't have any place to live and had been living with Mark, Peggy, and Skip, her children, for quite some time. I knew that this wasn't the best situation for her and began to pray about it. I asked Jesus to help find a permanent home for her. I also asked the Lord to help provide a means of income for her since she didn't have any money of her own. A few days after I prayed, the Lord gave me an answer to my prayer. I was talking with my next-door neighbor about this situation and she told me that she knew of a new program through the Metropolitan Housing Authority for low-income housing. She thought Mark's mother would probably qualify for a low-income apartment, and suggested that I investigate this option. In addition, she thought I should also contact Social Security for assistance.

I knew this was an answer to my prayers, so I began to investigate these options. I called the Metropolitan Housing Authority and the Department of Social Security and asked them what would be required in order for a person to qualify for their programs. I was told that I needed the death certificate of Stella's first husband, and needed to be able to prove that Stella had no other means of income or support from anyone else. I could prove that Stella had no income but I knew that legally Stella was still married to Mark's stepfather.

THOMAS MARK ZIEBOLD

Mark's stepfather had left Stella some time after they had been married but they hadn't been legally divorced.

I knew I had to find out where Mark's stepfather was so that I could prove that he was no longer providing a means of support for Stella. I had no idea where to begin this search and neither did Mark or anybody else. I prayed to Jesus that we might be led to find the whereabouts of Mark's stepfather.

My prayer was answered. It was amazing how God opened doors for us and guided us so that we might find Mark's stepfather quickly. I can't remember exactly how we tracked him down, but I know that the search was much easier than I had anticipated it would be. We found that he had been living with his daughter in Kentucky. Furthermore, Stella informed us that they had established a will together shortly after they were married, and that this will had never been changed. I contacted the daughter in Kentucky only to find that she was very evasive. She didn't want to answer any of my questions regarding her father.

She did, however, indicate that her father had lived with her and that he had passed away some time ago. I informed her that all I wanted from her was a copy of her father's death certificate so that I could prove that Stella had no means of supporting herself and was not being supported by anyone else. The daughter refused to give me the requested copy of the death certificate. I had a feeling that she was concerned that I was going to sue for whatever had been left of her father's estate after he had passed away. She knew that I had a copy of the will that had been put in place between Stella and her father, and was afraid that my call was a prelude to a court battle.

I informed the daughter many times that I wanted the copy of the death certificate only in order to prove that Stella had no means of support and that I had no interest in her father's estate, but she continued to be evasive and wouldn't provide a copy of her father's death certificate. I hung up the phone with no resolution. It seemed I had run into a brick wall.

I didn't let this discourage me, however, because I had been working in an attorney's office prior to the birth of the twins. I had remained fairly close with the attorneys, so I contacted one of them and asked what I should do about this situation. We had a letter written from his law firm requesting the death certificate. I tried this tactic but the daughter still refused to provide a copy of her father's death certificate. Again, I contacted my attorney and asked him what I should do. He indicated that he would help me out. He wrote a letter informing the daughter that she was to appear in court. He informed the daughter that her refusal to provide her father's death certificate had left us no option but to sue for the proceeds of her father's estate. He informed the daughter that we had a copy of Stella's will and that she was required to provide a copy of her father's death certificate. He informed her that failure to provide her father's death certificate would be a criminal offense and that she could be held liable for contempt of court.

A court hearing was set, and I had collected all of the required papers that would allow us to litigate this court case on behalf of Stella. I placed all of these important documents in a drawer within a chest in our dining room. It seemed we had everything we needed to litigate the case and provide some income for Mark's mother.

About a week prior to the court date the house caught on fire. The fire broke out at night, so we were all upstairs. I ran into the twin's room to get Tom out of bed. Mom had already taken Tami downstairs. There was very heavy smoke in the house. The smoke in the upstairs was so thick that I placed a blanket over Tom's head, so that he wouldn't breathe the smoke into his lungs. I ran downstairs, crossed the living room floor and went out the front door of the house.

Someone else must have called the fire department because trucks were already pulling up to the house as I was leaving. I thanked God that the firefighters had arrived so quickly. I had no time to waste though, because I knew that we had important papers in the dining room of the house. We needed those papers in order to litigate Stella's court case. The fire looked pretty bad so I rushed over to my neighbor's house and called our church prayer chain from there. I informed the prayer chain that our house was on fire and that the fire looked pretty bad. I asked them to pray for one thing. I didn't really care about the rest of the house but I asked them to make sure to pray that the dining room didn't burn. I told them that I had important papers in the dining room and that it must not burn!

The fire was very severe. I was told by some of the firemen, after the blaze had been extinguished, that the fire was so intense that one of their trucks had sustained severe heat damage because it had been parked too close to the house. Another fireman told me that he was amazed that I was able to exit the house in the manner in which I had.

He indicated that when his firemen tried to enter the house through the same door that I had exited, only moments before, they could not enter that door of the house. He indicated that the living room floor had completely collapsed and it was his opinion that I had walked across a carpet that had no floor under it. He said that it was a miracle that both of us were alive. There was also evidence in the aftermath of the fire that showed how intense it must have been. My mother had a diamond-banded watch in a metal jewelry case. The metal jewelry box had melted and the diamonds from the watch band were found encrusted in the melted metal case. This had been an extremely hot fire!

The amazing thing was that the dining room of the house remained relatively untouched by the fire. It was close to Christmastime and the tree that had been in our dining room was still green! In addition, the wax on the candles of the dining room table hadn't melted! How was it that the fire was so hot that it melted a metal jewelry case and damaged a fire truck outside of the house, but didn't melt the wax in the candles on the dining room table? When you really think about it there is but one explanation; this was a miracle. God protected that room throughout the fire so that it wouldn't burn. The adjacent rooms on either side of the dining room were completely destroyed by fire, but the dining room itself was virtually untouched by the flames. We also found the legal papers that we had been praying for without a mark on them. They didn't have any water damage or smoke damage! The documents were perfectly legible! It was as if God had placed his hand over that room in our house and said, "This room will not burn."

With the legal papers in hand we were able to litigate Stella's court case and were able to obtain a place for her to live and a means of support for her. It is amazing that, as intense as this fire was, one room was spared. It just so happened that the room that was spared was the exact same room we were praying for. If you are having a hard time convincing yourself that this was coincidental there is a very good reason for that — nothing about this fire was coincidental. Nothing happened by chance. All of the other rooms were completely destroyed except for the dining room. Rooms adjacent to the dining room were completely destroyed by the flames. I talked to the firemen and they indicated that they had never seen anything like this fire. They said it was one of the most intense fires they had ever encountered (certainly for a residential home anyway) and that the house should have been completely destroyed. They had no explanation for why the dining room was untouched by the fire. This was yet another example of God's quick answers to prayer in my life.

More than 20 years later Mark and I took a vacation. Mark and I began talking with a gentleman sitting next to us at one of the locations we were visiting. I found out that he had been a fire chief in one of the suburbs of Cincinnati. I began telling him this story about the miraculous fire on Blanche Avenue. He said that he had heard about that fire, and said the fire is somewhat legendary at the firehouse where he worked. He asked me if I knew about the lady who had carried the baby over a carpet that had no floor underneath it. I told him that I was that lady and showed him a picture of my son. Tom has since graduated from the University of Michigan-Flint and is married with children of his own. We had a very interesting conversation about the fire and the way Jesus has worked in my life.

The following pictures were taken after the fire. The sketchy black and white photographs were taken with a Polaroid camera. The first picture represents a view looking into the dining room. The chest that is depicted here (with the drawers removed) was the chest that contained the important legal documents that I was praying for. As a point of comparison, the second picture (next page) shows the living room. This was the room adjacent to the dining room. You can see in this picture the floor has completely collapsed. This was the room that I walked across when exiting the house.

The HEALING
of MY COLON

Within a period of about two years I had seen my father die of pneumonia, my family's finances destroyed by the fire on Blanche Avenue, and my mother die of a heart attack. My uncle, who was a trusted figurehead, had also died shortly after my mother. The loss of my mother was the most difficult for me to bear. I was so close with her. We did everything together. She was like a best friend, and had guided me though many difficult situations in life. It was incredibly hard to handle when she was taken from me so young in her life and so suddenly. I felt more alone and lost than at any previous time in my life. To make matters worse, Mark and I were having some problems of our own. Our relationship was going through some rocky times and this added stress to an already difficult situation. I was still, however, very active in church and I had a very solid relationship with the Holy Spirit.

I knew that God was well aware of all of the difficult circumstances of my life. I knew that he was in complete control of everything I was experiencing. I found comfort in the fact that the Bible promises that God will not permit anything to occur within a Christian's life that he or she cannot handle. I also knew that oftentimes we are permitted to face difficult circumstances in order to draw us closer to our heavenly Father and build true Christian character within us. I had full trust in God and leaned heavily on him through prayer throughout these difficult times.

My mother and father instilled a belief in me during my childhood years that it was bad to show emotion. They told me that I should never cry and that I should always maintain control over my emotions. My mother had always said that it made others around me uncomfortable when I showed my emotions. I remember when Terry, my first husband, died. My mother had told me not to cry. As a result of the way I was raised I had always kept all of my emotions bottled up inside. In addition, ever since I was a little girl I always had problems with my colon. Whenever I got sick, or nervous I would get colitis. It seemed that I would always get nervous right before the next school year and I would always come down with a case of colitis right before school began. The problem got so bad that by the time I was in high school I was diagnosed with acute colitis. It was awful.

The occurrence of so many terrible events in such a short period of time had a severe impact on me both physically and emotionally. I really felt, however, that I was handling the situation well. I had been asking for God's guidance through prayer and had been including God in all of the difficult situations that I encountered. In addition, I was seeing the Holy Spirit provide for the needs of my family and I fully trusted that he would help me handle everything that I was faced with. I had total confidence in God.

I felt I had everything under control up until the point when my colon became completely nonfunctional. I found that I was in an extreme amount of pain and could barely use the bathroom. I was so horribly ill that everyone in the family was really concerned about me. In fact, my sister called my family doctor about the situation.

She informed him about a lot of personal details about my life. I suppose she felt that he needed to be aware of everything that was going on in my life in order to treat me effectively. She informed him of all the recent deaths in the family and the fact that my first marriage with Terry had been an abusive relationship.

My problems had been so severe that I was seeing my family physician three times a week. He and I had gotten to know each other quite well during this time in my life because of all of my health problems. We had become close friends. I felt he was a great doctor and a true blessing to me during this time in my life. He was an old-time practitioner who helped me through some difficult times. In fact, I can remember one time when Tom was cutting teeth and had a horrible fever. I couldn't get the fever to break. I called him and told him that I was having a difficult time.

I told him that I didn't have a car and I didn't have any money. He told me to get a taxi and bring Tom into his office. He paid for the taxi and we broke the fever together . He was that type of doctor — an extremely nice and caring gentleman. He determined that I was clinically depressed and placed me on all sorts of medications that were supposed to relieve my depression. After my sister spoke to him he gave me a call. He asked me to come into his office for an appointment as soon as possible. At the appointment, he told me that my sister had made him aware of some things that I had never shared with him and that this information was crucial for my treatment. He wanted to talk to me about alternative forms of treatment. He had a difficult time understanding why I had chosen not to share these incidents of my life with him.

I told him that I didn't really think that my personal life history was important to share with him. He responded by saying that every aspect of a person's life is important when treating a medical illness. He said that maybe this was the secret to unlocking my colon and recommended psychiatric help for me. This was the first time in my life that I had ever undergone psychiatric counseling.

The psychiatrist didn't prescribe drugs but I found the counseling sessions to be very helpful. The sessions helped me analyze my personality. The counseling sessions helped me deal with life. My colon, however, still wasn't healing. It was locked up and wasn't getting any better. In fact, it finally got to the point where the doctors thought I was going to need to have a colostomy. I was young, about the age of 30, and I didn't want a colostomy. I was continuously praying about my colon. I had many friends in church praying for me as well, but my colon just didn't seem to be getting any better. I was in so much pain that I began to get discouraged, but I knew that people were praying for me and I had faith that God would heal me.

One day I had to take our dog to the veterinarian. Beufort was my children's first dog. He was a very mild-tempered dog and was great with Tami and Tom. We all loved him and he fit perfectly into our family. He especially loved Tami. He used to sleep with her every night. He really was the nicest dog. For some reason the veterinarian took him into the back room to examine him. I couldn't see Beufort or the veterinarian but apparently Beufort bit the veterinarian during the examination. He bit him hard enough to draw blood and the veterinarian was extremely upset.

He informed me that I had a vicious dog and said I needed to have him put to sleep. To this day I don't know what that veterinarian did to Beufort in that examining room but I know he must have done something to cause him to bite. I later found out that the veterinarian had a nervous breakdown soon after this incident and I have little doubt that he did something to cause Beufort to lash out and bite him.

The thought of putting Beufort to sleep broke my heart and I began to cry. I had never really cried before in my life so this became a real emotional outlet for me. I went home and I cried like you wouldn't believe. I cried for hours and the tears just kept flowing. I had an appointment with my psychiatrist that day and I was barely able to stop crying in time for my appointment. In fact, I was still very much upset at my appointment. My psychiatrist and I talked about my crying and my tears. I told him that I had never cried that much before in my life. I told him I hadn't cried when I lost either my mother or my father. I hadn't cried when I lost Terry either. The doctor told me that in order for people to be healed they must release their emotions.

He said that it is very important to have emotional outlets. He pointed out that tears were a form of emotional release and he felt that I had cried so much over this incident because I had never released my emotions before. He said that when people don't release their emotions, their bodies hold onto them and this oftentimes causes their bodies to attack their weakest areas. In my case this was my colon. As a result of my inability to show and release my emotions, my colon was getting sicker and sicker.

This was an incredible realization in my life. My life, up to this point, resembled a duck. If you look at a duck on the surface of the water, he looks as if he's gliding effortlessly across the top of the water. It isn't until you look underneath the surface of the water that you see his little legs paddling and paddling to move him in the water. As for me, I was putting a good outward appearance on my emotions, but I was really struggling internally to deal with them and this was causing many of my health problems. The tears started a cleansing and healing process within my body, but my colon still wasn't healing. I was, however, learning to deal with life and to show my emotions instead of keeping them all bottled up inside.

I realized that I needed to get a handle on my health problems so I decided to give myself a project to work on that would serve as a good emotional outlet for me. I started to strip and re-do all of the woodwork in my kitchen. I wanted to bring my kitchen back to its original wood tones, so I began the project. This was a big job but I really wanted to change the appearance of my kitchen. I listened to the radio as I worked. There was a radio station in Cincinnati that played really good religious music. It was the type of religious music that had a quick beat to it and it really made me feel good. I enjoyed the music while I worked on the kitchen. After a period of time the radio station started broadcasting a faith healing program. I knew the station aired this program but I had never believed in faith healing over the radio. I felt that the person behind the michrophone could say anything and there was never any proof that he or she was actually healing anybody. I believed that faith healers were charlatans.

I was in so much pain, however, that I really didn't feel like getting up off the floor to change the station, so I just listened to it as I worked.

At one point during the program the person on the radio made a statement that really made me angry. He said, "You, young lady with the colon problem who is listening to this program, the Lord has just healed your colon!" This made me angry because I felt that this person had a lot of nerve saying that! I had a colon problem and I really didn't think this radio healer had any business giving people false hope. I believed these "healers" were just saying this because people were sending them a lot of money, but they really weren't healing anybody. I thought this was a farce. I mean, honestly, anyone could be listening to the radio with a colon problem. How would anyone know if someone was actually healed?

As this thought process was running through my mind the radio healer came back on the air and said, "You, young lady out in radio land, the Lord has just informed me that you are being very skeptical but he wants you to know that he has healed you." He did this about three or four times and every time I got madder and madder. I thought, "How can you give this person such blind hope? That is really cruel and really mean!" Then, all of the sudden I was stripping the varnish from the cabinets and I thought, "Hmm, I feel pretty good. I'm not in a lot of pain. In fact, I haven't felt this good in a long time." Just then I got up and I felt my stomach. My stomach was soft for the first time in what must have been months.

Ever since I had been experiencing these colon problems my stomach had been as hard as a rock, but now it was soft. I wondered if I was the person the radio announcer had been talking about. I had been ranting and raving at this radio healer and now it looked like I might actually be the person that he was talking about. I felt horrible that I had expressed such a bad attitude toward the radio healer.

I made an appointment with my doctor to have him check my colon. He examined me and said that he was amazed! I told him about the radio program and asked him if he thought it was possible that I might have been healed. I told him that I had not been receptive to what the man was saying over the radio. In fact, I hadn't even believed him. He said that he didn't know what radio program I had been listening to but it appeared that I had been healed. He told me that something definitely had happened and that there was a noticeable difference in my colon. He ran some additional tests and found that my colon had been completely healed.

Acts 3:16 says, "By faith in the name Jesus, this man whom you see and know was made strong. It is Jesus' name and the faith that comes through him that has given the complete healing to him, as you can all see."

This is another example of God's amazing love. At the time I was healed I didn't even believe in the person who was telling me that I had been healed. I wasn't receptive to it at all. In fact, I was extremely angry with the gentleman who was telling me that I had been healed. Despite all of my disbelief Jesus healed me in a miraculous manner. I had been praying for quite some time for the healing of my colon. When the Holy Spirit finally healed me I didn't recognize it right away. I had become so angry with the radio healer that I failed to recognize that he was talking about me and that the Lord had provided an amazing response to my prayers.

The HEALING *o f* *a* LITTLE GIRL

I became involved in a women's Bible study group at church. While I was listening to the Bible study a man suddenly burst into the room and interrupted our fellowship group. The man said that the church had just received a phone call from the hospital. There was a little girl who was in desperate condition. He asked us to pray for her immediately and said that if the Holy Spirit didn't do something for the girl that she would most likely die very soon. The man explained that the little girl had contracted some sort of flu-like illness. It had turned into a very serious condition. The girl had become paralyzed below the neck. The paralysis had started in her feet and moved up her spinal column. She was now bedridden and unable to move any part of her body below her neck. In addition, the girl had been placed on a respirator since she could no longer sustain breathing on her own. The man who interrupted our Bible study said the girl couldn't hold on for much longer and, unless the Holy Spirit intervened, she wouldn't likely make it through the night.

At that moment we broke up the Bible study and the entire group headed down to the church sanctuary to pray. We started praying that the Lord would touch that girl's body. We prayed that the Lord would heal this little girl and make her whole again. While we were praying for the girl the same man who had interrupted our prayer meeting came back into the sanctuary. He said that he had just received another phone call from the hospital and that the little girl had been healed! This was very shortly after we had started praying – an instant answer from God!

He said that the paralysis had completely gone and the girl was no longer in danger of dying. In fact, he said that the girl had been healed so completely the doctors were considering taking her off of the respirators because they believed that she could breathe on her own again. Of course this miraculous turnaround in the girl's prognosis completely baffled the doctors. They didn't know what to think and had no explanation for this type of miraculous improvement in the girl's condition. We, of course, knew that this was the Holy Spirit at work. The Holy Spirit healed the girl. There is no other explanation. Her paralysis was completely gone and she had been made whole again.

This healing was so complete that by the next day, when the mother went to visit her daughter in the hospital she found the little girl sitting up in bed. The girl was able to feed herself. Not only that, but the girl was able to get out of bed and walk for her mother. This was truly an awesome and miraculous turnaround in her condition when you consider the fact that only a few hours prior she had been completely unable to move any part of her body below the neck and couldn't even breathe on her own! This is the awesome power of the Holy Spirit!

Mathew 8:5-13 says the following:

> [5] *When Jesus had entered Capernaum, a centurion came to him, asking for help.* [6] *"Lord," he said, "my servant lies at home paralyzed and in terrible suffering."*

⁷Jesus said to him, "I will go and heal him."

⁸The centurion replied, "Lord, I do not deserve to have you come under my roof. But just say the word, and my servant will be healed. ⁹For I myself am a man under authority, with soldiers under me. I tell this one, 'Go,' and he goes; and that one 'Come,' and he comes, I say to my servant, 'Do this,' and he does it.'

¹⁰When Jesus heard this, he was astonished and said to those following him, "I tell you the truth, I have not found anyone in Israel with such great faith. ¹¹I say to you that many will come from the east and the west, and will take their places at the feast with Abraham, Isaac, and Jacob in the kingdom of Heaven. ¹²But the subjects of the kingdom will be thrown outside, into the darkness, where there will be weeping and gnashing of teeth."

¹³Then Jesus said to the centurion, "Go! It will be done just as you believed it would." And his servant was healed at the very hour.

This set of scriptures is very similar to what happened with the girl in the hospital room that night. Nobody had laid hands on her. Nobody was around her when she was healed, other than the medical staff at the hospital. Friends prayed from a distance and Jesus healed this girl from a distance, just as he had done for the centurion's servant. It was the faith and power of the Holy Spirit that healed the girl. There is no other explanation for the miraculous turnaround in her condition.

T h e
G O L D F I S H

While my children were very young I started instilling Christian beliefs and values within their lives. Each night our family would sit down and we would share a time together that we referred to as "Devotions." This time was spent in the word of God teaching my children the stories of the Bible. Each night we would spend at least fifteen to thirty minutes reading stories from the Bible and learning about God's word. We always had our devotional time just before bedtime. Oftentimes I felt myself wondering if Tami and Tom really understood the stories of the Bible or their importance. Sometimes I wondered if they weren't just asking questions in order to stall before we sent them to bed. I knew, however, that these beliefs and values were important to my children and that God would work to make sure they understood everything they needed to know. What was important was that we spent time in God's word and understood how important the Bible was.

When my children were about four or five years of age I started teaching them about how important prayer is in our lives. I told them that the Bible says that wherever there are two or more gathered in God's name, there he will be also. Mathew 18:20 (NLT) says, "Where two or three gather together, because they are mine, I am there among them."

I told them that God always listened to our prayers and made a promise to us that he would hear our prayers, no matter what we were praying for. I taught my children how to pray and each night we would say a short prayer together before we went to bed.

We always had pets in our house. When my children were growing up they had dogs, hamsters, and goldfish. We never had cats, though, because Mark never liked cats. About the same time that I was trying to teach my children about the importance of prayer their pet goldfish died. Tom thought the goldfish looked thirsty and had decided to give the goldfish some Coca-Cola to drink. I'm not exactly sure how much soda he actually dumped into the bowl but I know it was enough to kill the goldfish. Tom apparently didn't grasp the concept that the goldfish was in an entire bowl full of water and could get a drink whenever it wanted. I still remember this day vividly. Both Tami and Tom came running to me yelling, "Mom, Mom, the goldfish is dead!" Sure enough, I went to the goldfish bowl and there it was, floating on top of the water completely lifeless. The fish wasn't moving at all. It was just laying there flat on top of the surface of the water, rolled over with its fat tummy up.

My first instinct was to give my children a quick lesson on life and death. I would couple this lesson with another quick lesson about why we don't give the goldfish Coca-Cola to drink. After these lessons in life I would flush the goldfish down the toilet. Parents face this type of problem all the time with any child who has a pet. Sooner or later the pet dies and the child needs to understand that things don't live forever.

My logic would have worked perfectly except that Tom looked up at me and said, "Mom, you have been teaching us about the power of prayer. I bet if we prayed to God for him to bring our goldfish back to life that he would do it." Instantly I knew that God would listen to our prayer to bring the goldfish back to life.

I knew that the life or death of this goldfish seemed like a petty thing to pray about but I also knew that God would show his glory to my children and answer their prayer to bring their pet goldfish back to life. I had been trying to instill a belief in my children that God is loving and that he listens to all of our prayers. I knew that the lessons I was trying to teach to my children were very important and I knew that God would use this as an opportunity to show my children an example of the power of prayer. Teaching a child that nothing lives forever is a relatively simple task. Trusting God to provide a lesson on the power of prayer and bring a dead goldfish back to life requires quite a bit more faith but I had no doubt that God would answer my children's prayer. I believe that God is quick to show us examples of his glory so that we may glorify him.

It's funny how a simple little sentence spoken by a five-year-old can change the entire situation. When my son asked me to pray for his pet goldfish I knew that God was providing an opportunity for me to show my children a true example of the power of prayer. Anyone thinking from a strictly logical standpoint would say that there was no way this dead fish was going to come back to life. Speaking from a position of faith, however, I was sure that God was providing this situation in order that my children might learn how powerful prayer could be.

I said my own short prayer before I prayed with my children. I knew that asking Jesus to bring a dead goldfish back to life wasn't the issue we were praying about. I knew that what we were really asking Jesus for was for him to show his glory so that my children would learn a valuable lesson. I knew that this wasn't a petty request and that Jesus would answer it. I prayed to Jesus, "Lord, I know the life of this fish seems like a petty request but it's extremely important to my children. It's also important to me that my children learn the lessons that I have been trying to teach to them about the power of prayer. Lord, if it be your will, I would ask that you please bring this dead goldfish back to life when my children and I pray together so that they will learn how powerful prayer can be." After I was done praying I knew that the decision to grant my children's prayer was in God's hands. I had absolute faith that he would answer their prayer.

I sat down with Tami and Tom and we prayed for the life of this dead little goldfish. After we were done praying that goldfish flicked his tail, turned over and swam. He had come back to life! This was a true miracle that God had performed. My children had learned an important lesson about the power of prayer, and their goldfish was brought back to life. As for me, I was awestruck. I wasn't in awe that Jesus had decided to grant our prayer, but each time I have been witness to a miracle I have been in awe of the glory of God! God is truly loving and caring and he won't hesitate to show his glory to his followers. I knew he had done far more on this day than simply bringing a pet goldfish back to life. I said another short prayer thanking Jesus for the miracle. From my perspective there are no "minor" miracles.

A miracle is a miracle, and there was no question in my mind that Jesus had performed a real miracle on behalf of my children's prayer request. Dead goldfish don't just come back to life on their own accord.

After I said a short prayer of thanks, I gave my children a brief lesson on life and death. I figured that it was also important that they understand that things didn't live forever and that oftentimes we need to say good-bye to our pets, or even our loved ones. What a joy to know that we have such a loving God that he would honor a request to bring a pet goldfish back to life! This miracle left a lasting impression.

Each time I talk about the power of prayer I think back to this simple little episode in my life. I learned an important lesson on this day, and it really bolstered my faith that Jesus hears our prayers attentively and doesn't hesitate to answer them. I never question the power of prayer.

Prayer is one of the most powerful gifts that God has provided to his followers. The Bible makes it clear that God has promised to listen to the prayers of his followers and will answer them without hesitation. The following verses provide some of the promises that God has made regarding the answering of prayers:

> *"Trust me in your times of trouble, and I will rescue you, and you will give me glory"*
> *(Ps. 50:15 NLT).*

> *"The earnest prayer of a righteous person has great power and wonderful results" (James 5:16 NLT).*

> *"I will answer them before they even call on me. While they are still talking to me about their needs, I will go ahead and answer their prayers"*
> *(Isa. 65:24 NLT).*

> *"If you stay joined to me and my words remain in you, you may ask any request you like, and it will be granted" (John 15:7 NLT).*

God does, however, reserve the right to answer our prayers in his own time. Never forget that God doesn't work the way humans work and he doesn't work on a human's timeline. He works in ways we don't understand and has his own schedule for your life. We can never fully comprehend God's timing, but we know that to him a thousand years is like a day and a day is like a thousand years. In other words, time has no meaning to God. He isn't limited by anything. There have been times in my life when I received an instant answer to prayer. There have been other times when I had to wait for God's answer to my prayers, and still others when God provided a simple answer of no. We must always remember that God has infinite wisdom and he always does what's in the best interest of his followers. Everything that is provided by God is perfect. Sometimes God's greatest blessings are prayers that he has chosen not to grant. We must have faith in God's infinite wisdom and goodness. We must be content to give everything to him through prayer and trust that he will provide what's ultimately best for us. Prayers are a true blessing provided by God; however, many Christians struggle with prayer and can become frustrated with it.

When we feel frustrated in our prayer lives it's important to remember that the Bible provides some insights about prayer that may prove helpful in removing our frustrations. First, we must remember that there are things in our lives that can interfere with the relationship that we have with God. For instance, Mark 11:24-26 (NLT) tells us the following:

> *Listen to me! You can pray for anything, and if you believe, you will have it. But when you are praying, first forgive anyone you are holding a grudge against, so that your Father in heaven will forgive your sins. But if you do not forgive, neither will your Father who is in heaven forgive your sins.*

This verse provides a clear indication that the failure to forgive someone who has done something against us can hinder the relationship that we have with God. Grudges have no place in the life of a Christian and can have an impact on our prayer lives. In addition, we must remember that it's not the words of our prayers, but our motives that are truly important to God. Proverbs 16:2 (NLT) tells us, "People may be pure in their own eyes, but the Lord examines their motives."

It's clear that God understands any hidden agenda or any selfish motives that we might have. Oftentimes we can get frustrated in our prayer lives because, in our flesh, we have a desire to sin. Our own selfish desires oftentimes become a barrier to our prayer lives.

God has made it clear in his promises regarding prayer that if Christians call upon him, have faith in him, and have pure motives that he will answer their prayer.

That doesn't necessarily mean that he will answer yes. It just means that he will listen to your prayers and answer them. If our lives are right in Christ, and our motives are pure, then I firmly believe that God has made promises to his followers that their prayers will be answered.

You should also remember that when God answers no to a prayer it doesn't always mean that your motives were selfish. An example of this can be seen in the life of Paul. Paul asked God three times to remove what he called a "thorn" in his flesh. Paul never described exactly what this was but it is clear that three times God answered no. Paul later explained that God had answered no three times because the "thorn" in Paul's flesh brought more glory to God through Paul's ministry and witness. Paul became comfortable with the fact that God wasn't going to take away the "thorn" in his flesh and even rejoiced that it brought more glory to God! When God's answer to your prayer is a refusal it can be frustrating, but bear in mind that you share good company with Paul. As long as you understand that God is in complete control, and has your best interest in mind it makes it a little easier to accept the refusal. God often permits difficult circumstances in our lives in order to build true Christian character within us. Just remember that God might be using a difficult circumstance in your life to draw you closer to him!

MARK'S LAYOFF *from* GENERAL MOTORS

After Tami and Tom went to school I decided to get a full-time job. I went to work for General Motors and worked out of the Oldsmobile Zone office in Cincinnati. I was a customer service representative responsible for handling investigations into customer complaints. I enjoyed working and my paycheck really helped Mark and me save quite a bit of money. Mark and I hadn't really grown accustomed to my salary so we were living well below our means. Mark always saved a lot of money so that we always had a fairly healthy reserve just in case something happened. Having survived the fire on Blanche Avenue we learned a valuable lesson about saving money and living below our means. We would soon come to realize the importance of saving our money during this time in our lives.

Mark was working for the Norwood Assembly Plant for General Motors in the 1980s. He had birth defects in his legs and was experiencing a lot of problems walking. He consulted a doctor and was informed he could no longer work in the production environment. The doctor told Mark that if he didn't get transferred into a job with much less walking he would soon be crippled. Mark notified General Motors of this and he was transferred out of the production environment. We both felt that it was good to get Mark out of the production environment because he was getting to the point where it was extremely painful for him to walk.

During the decade of the 1980s the American automotive industry was going through some very difficult times. A terrible economic downturn had resulted in severe cutbacks and layoffs by General Motors. Norwood was one of the older assembly plants operated by General Motors. During the 1980s the plant produced two sports cars with very little market demand, the Camaro and the Firebird. As a result, many of the people with whom Mark worked requested transfers to other locations. They realized that the Norwood Assembly Plant was a prime candidate to be closed by General Motors. Mark and I, however, were in no position to leave Cincinnati. One of our closest relatives, who had been like a father to Mark, had started showing signs of some serious health problems. As a result, we decided we needed to remain in Cincinnati in order to help him and his wife cope with his medical needs.

In addition to our relatives' health problems, Mark and I miscalculated the depth of the economic downturn. We both thought it wouldn't last that long. We had saved a lot of money and figured that if Mark got laid off for a short period of time we could survive without much of a problem. Mark also had quite a bit of tenure built up with General Motors so he thought he would be protected against a layoff. We were also both certain that people with less experience would be laid off before Mark. Due to all of these factors Mark didn't seek a transfer out of the Norwood Assembly Plant. It turned out, however, despite having more than eighteen years' experience with General Motors, Mark was laid off.

General Motors had retained many people that had only two years of tenure but, because Mark had transferred out of the production environment, he was laid off. His position wasn't considered a "mission critical" resource, which made him expendable.

Mark's documented medical condition precluded a move back into the production environment, where he would have been more insulated from the layoffs. The company couldn't give him the option to move back into the production environment because it likely would have meant serious medical problems for Mark. I can tell you that Mark would have gladly faced the medical problems rather than face the prospect of a layoff. Unfortunately, this wasn't an option and Mark lost his job.

In addition to losing his job he was forced to pull all of his money out of his stock purchase program. I believe this practice is now illegal but pulling all of our money out of the stock purchase program forced us to pay a huge amount in taxes that we otherwise would not have had to pay. This was a hard financial hit. We still had quite a bit of money in savings, though, and we thought we could survive the layoff so we weren't overly concerned. I felt so sorry for Mark. He has always been a very proud person and has taken great pride in his ability to provide for his family. During this time in his life Mark hunted for jobs every day but there simply weren't that many jobs available and the jobs that were available were never a good fit. Mark was willing to take a much more menial job than his experience would have otherwise provided just to earn an income, but when he interviewed for those types of jobs he was consistently told that he was overqualified.

Employers didn't want to hire Mark because they were afraid he would leave soon after he was hired. They knew that if Mark got called back to work for General Motors he would leave. Companies simply didn't want to hire him given the fact that he probably wouldn't work for them long.

General Electric contacted Mark several times about a supervisory position. They even offered Mark a position, but he couldn't accept the job offers because they required him to sign a contract stating that he wouldn't go back to work for General Motors. Mark couldn't sign the contract because he had more than eighteen years of tenure with General Motors. He was eligible to receive retirement benefits and he was in no position to give this up. Mark was very depressed during the time of his layoff.

During the layoff the situation got really bad in my workplace as well. A new manager was running the office and he and I didn't get along very well. I remember one incident specifically. It was Secretary's Day and my manager had decided that he was going to take all the secretaries out for lunch. He told me that I would cover the floor and that he would make it up to me on a later day. I tended the phones while everyone else was taken out to lunch. They were gone a long time, but I handled everything fine. The day came when he was going to take me out to lunch. I got ready for work and dressed up nicely because he had told me that he was going to take me out to a really nice restaurant. When the time came for him to take me out to lunch he never stopped by or called me.

It got to be several hours after we were supposed to go to lunch when he finally called me. When he did call he informed me that he wasn't going to take me out to lunch and, in fact, had never intended to take me out to lunch. I responded to him by saying that it was okay. I told him that I understood that he was busy and that I was a "big girl" and could handle lunch on my own. This incident crushed me, though, and I had a hard time keeping my emotions in check while at work. This was just one example of the mean and nasty things he used to do to me. It got to the point where I dreaded going into work every day. I was so emotionally upset about going into work that my feet and hands would sweat. I dreaded facing my boss and coworkers.

I had also started working two jobs in order to help make ends meet during Mark's layoff. I worked a second job for Mary Kay cosmetics and I really didn't need the added stress of a mean and nasty boss in my life, but that was the situation I was faced with. To make matters worse for Mark, he knew the situations that were going on in my office. I used to come home and pray about it every night. On one occasion I came home and I told everyone that I didn't want to be disturbed. I told them that I was going up to my room to pray and not to disturb me under any circumstances.

I used to pray to the Holy Spirit that he would give me strength not to return his mean and nasty behavior with the same type of behavior. I prayed that he would give me the strength to love him and show the love of the Holy Spirit through me even under these difficult circumstances. One night when I was praying I received a visitor. Tami and Tom disturbed me, even though I had asked them not to.

They said a friend from church had come to visit. She had stopped by the house unannounced and told me that she was driving around and had the feeling that she needed to stop by the house. She prayed with me that night and really made me feel much better, but the situation at work wasn't getting any better. This made things hard for Mark because he knew, while he wasn't working, I was in no position to leave my job. We needed my income and I was being placed in a situation where I had to endure terrible treatment.

Finally I received a break from my boss. He had a medical condition that forced him to be out of the office for an extended period of time. During that time I was performing his duties because Oldsmobile didn't want to hire someone else on a temporary basis. They felt I was more than qualified to do his job for a limited period of time. During the time he was off work our department didn't miss a beat. I found that I really did have a lot of great people who worked around me. They were highly qualified people and really helped me perform his job functions. When he returned to the office, however, matters got worse for me. He wasn't happy with the fact that I had excelled at his job. In fact, he told me that he was going to make life a "living hell" for me until I decided to quit my job. I told him that I was in no position to quit my job and that he wasn't going to force me out! A few days after I had this conversation with my boss I became aware of a position that had suddenly opened up in the Chevrolet Zone Office. Apparently, the secretary for the Chevrolet Zone Office had suddenly died of a heart attack and they needed to fill the position quickly. I felt horrible for the lady who had died, but I really wanted out of my current position.

The position was a few levels below my job classification but I found out that I could request to be "bumped down" a few levels and put in for a transfer to that office. I found out that my current pay status would remain unchanged but my top-level pay scale would be decreased due to "bumping down" two levels. I really wanted out of this situation so I entered a transfer request to the Chevrolet Zone Office.

It turned out that the Chevrolet Zone Office wanted to hire me, but Oldsmobile was unwilling to let me go and blocked the transfer. This was very discouraging to me because I really wanted to get away from my boss, but I had to have an income. During this time I was working a lot of overtime. My boss refused to allow me to take any vacation even though I was entitled to it. His treatment grew worse and worse to the point that I felt I had to use the open-door policy.

I invoked the open-door policy. The policy was meant to protect employees from physical or mental harassment. This policy allowed an employee to talk directly to representatives within the Human Resources department of General Motors. The policy was supposed to ensure that any alleged incident of harassment was to be investigated and taken seriously. I found this to be of no help. I quickly found out that the managers at General Motors looked out for their fellow managers during this era. Nobody stood up for me and it seemed that my boss had won another major battle. Having won this battle he became even more abusive toward me. He believed that he had unlimited reign to do whatever he wanted to me since the open-door policy had failed. I really felt like I was in a hopeless situation.

One day another manager asked me to meet him for lunch. During lunch he informed me that he was aware of what had taken place. He felt horrible that the open-door policy had done nothing for me. He told me that he was going to "go to bat" for me and wanted to get me transferred to his department as his personal secretary. In order to make the transfer work, however, I had to take the first step of reducing my level because the secretarial position that I would transfer into was two levels lower than my current position. I thought about the benefits of this move and went ahead and requested to be "bumped down" two levels. I really thought that, by reducing my level, it would open an opportunity for me to work as his secretary. Bumping down a few levels was worth it as long as it allowed me to work for a different manager. This meeting gave me some hope, once again, of getting out of my difficult situation.

After I reduced my level, however, I found that my situation grew even worse. When I reduced my level, my manager promoted his secretary into my previous position. In addition, the other manager, that had met me for lunch, was unable to hire me as his personal secretary. As a result, I remained an employee of my existing manager, but at a much lower level. If I had thought things were bad before, they just got worse! Not only was I reduced two levels but now I was serving as his personal secretary! Again, he had won a major battle. He had been telling me, all along, that he was going to get my job. To him this was a great victory because I had quit my job and was now working as his personal secretary. I really felt the situation was hopeless but I continued to pray and I continued to ask for God's guidance and strength to show love through my actions at work. I really didn't want to be mean and nasty to my manager but it was becoming increasingly difficult to maintain a positive attitude at work and at home.

During this time the Holy Spirit provided for a lot of our family needs. My sister's husband found all sorts of odd jobs for Mark to do. He knew that Mark needed the income, and he asked Mark to help out whenever he found work. These were strange jobs. For one job Mark ripped up old railroad ties in the middle of winter. I'm sure the job was terrible but it was money coming into the house and Mark was happy to do any job at this time in his life. I can remember another occasion when one of Mark's old friends came to the house. He dropped off a load of groceries and told me that he just had a feeling that he needed to drop these groceries off at the house.

These examples showed me that the Holy Spirit was still very much involved in our lives during these difficult years. Despite Mark taking odd jobs here and there, our money was quickly running out. This had been an extremely long layoff and we had almost completely depleted our savings account. We had decided when Mark got laid off that we weren't going to sell our house in order to reduce our expenses. We didn't expect the layoff to last as long as it did and we wanted to keep Tami and Tom in the same school system. As a result we found that we weren't able to survive on my income. The situation got so bad that Mark and I both realized that we would need to either borrow money from our relatives in order to make the house payments or call our creditors and inform them that we could no longer make our house payments. We were facing very serious decisions within a matter of a few short months.

We continued to pray about our financial situation and God answered our prayers. Mark was called back to work at the Norwood Assembly Plant one month prior to our inability to make our house payment. This was truly a blessing. We still had a lot of financial problems. We had completely depleted our savings account, but Mark was finally working again!

Romans 8:28 says, "And we know that in all things God works for the good of those who love him, who have been called according to his purpose."

I believe that the Holy Spirit used this difficult time in our lives to teach Mark and me some important lessons in life. He taught us that he was still in control of everything and that he had not abandoned us. He taught us that we could trust the Lord even when times looked hopeless.

RELOCATION
to MICHIGAN

Soon after Mark was called back to work he knew that something was wrong. He could see that the assembly plant wasn't ordering any materials for the following production year. He knew this was a sign that GM was going to close the assembly plant, and he immediately started looking for a transfer to a different location.

I was really hoping that Mark would get transferred to a different location quickly because my boss and I were continuing to have problems getting along with each other. I really felt it was in my best interest to "change scenery" if at all possible. Mark and I started looking around for alternative geographic locations. Many of our friends had transferred to Dayton, which was only about thirty to forty miles north of Cincinnati. We didn't like that location, however, because we weren't comfortable with the school systems. We felt it was important, however, to remain close to Cincinnati due to our relatives' health problems. We wanted to be in a position to help whenever it became necessary. General Motors had just built a new assembly plant in Lake Orion, Michigan. Mark and I looked into that geographic location and it was ideal. We decided to focus our attention on the Orion Assembly Plant for Mark's transfer. Orion was about five hours north of Cincinnati, so it would provide the opportunity to get home to Cincinnati on very short notice. In addition, we had heard that there were several good school systems in the areas surrounding the assembly plant.

Mark and I traveled to Lake Orion so that we could check out the area firsthand. I had a lot of vacation time saved because my boss refused to let me take any previously during the year. This turned out to be a real blessing because I had no problem taking time off late in the year for our trip to Lake Orion. Mark and I really liked the area. It was a rural community that offered some very nice areas to live. As part of our visit to Lake Orion, Mark dropped his resume off at the Orion Assembly Plant.

He really fell in love with the assembly plant. It was an enormous plant. General Motors had built a few extremely modern assembly plants in order to compete with the Japanese automakers. The assembly plant was an instrumental part of GM's strategic objective. In fact, they referred to these assembly plants as their "battleship" plants. The assembly plant was about as beautiful as an assembly plant could be. It was air conditioned and had special floors that helped reduce the shock while walking during a production run. This was ideal for Mark's legs. When Mark dropped his resume off at the assembly plant, however, he was told that they wouldn't be hiring for at least six months to a year. I really thought that we might be stuck in our current situation for at least another six months. We just had to hope that the Norwood Assembly Plant wasn't closed before we could get Mark transferred to Orion.

Neither Mark nor I realized it when we dropped his resume off, but two of Mark's previous managers at Norwood had transferred to the Orion Assembly Plant. One had been Mark's manager during the time we experienced the fire on Blanche Avenue.

In fact, he was the manager who had sent Mark home so that he could take care of his family during the Christmas holidays. The other manager had worked with Mark during the "wildcat" strike in Norwood, when Mark was transferred to Ypsilanti. Both of them considered Mark to be an outstanding supervisor, and they had moved into very prominent positions within the production area of the Orion Assembly Plant. Apparently, one of them found Mark's resume and requested that he be brought in for an immediate interview.

Within a few months of our visit to Lake Orion Mark had been hired as a production supervisor at the Orion Assembly Plant. I have no doubt that God was preparing a place for us years in advance and had been looking out for us the entire time Mark was laid off. I firmly believe that the Lord had made sure those managers were placed in a situation that would allow them to help Mark obtain his transfer out of the Norwood Assembly Plant. Not only that, but the Lord really found the most suitable environment for us. The assembly plant had good school systems surrounding it and it was a brand new facility. God even paid attention to details such as the floors in the assembly plant to make them easier for Mark's legs.

The assembly plant was also critical to the strategic objectives of General Motors, so it was highly unlikely that it would be closed any time soon. It really provided the best long-term security for our family. To this day I'm amazed at how God works! I was also very relieved to know that I would be getting a new job! I informed my boss that I needed to obtain a transfer within General Motors as a result of Mark's new position. I filled out my transfer papers and submitted them to Human Resources. Weeks went by, however, and I wasn't receiving any calls for interviews. Finally I received a call from an extremely nice man in Michigan. He asked me if I was looking for a transfer to Michigan. He told me that he had come across my resume but that it had never been sent through the proper channels. He informed me that nobody within the organization was aware that I was looking for jobs in Michigan. He was such a nice man that he stayed with me on the phone and provided numerous numbers and names of people working within personnel departments in Michigan. As a result of working through him I finally started getting calls for interviews in Michigan.

The fact that my boss never let me take a vacation really worked to my advantage, once again, now that Mark had been transferred to Michigan. It gave me the opportunity to take a lot of time off so that I could interview in Michigan and look for a place to live. I really feel that the Lord permitted my stressful work situation because he knew there would be a benefit later. After Mark got transferred he moved into an apartment in Troy, Michigan. Tami, Tom, and I were living in Cincinnati so I could sell our home in Cincinnati. We drove up every weekend to see Mark and hunt for houses. One day my boss called me into his office. He informed me that he had filled my position and that my replacement was going to start working in a matter of a few weeks. He informed me that once my replacement started working I would be let go. I was very upset about this because Mark and I still hadn't fully recovered from his long layoff. Now I was being faced with a layoff and I had no idea how long it might be before I found a new job in Michigan. In addition, I didn't know if this termination would affect my transfer request within General Motors.

I called Mark and asked him if my manager was permitted to replace me in this manner. I really didn't think that he could replace me simply because my husband had been transferred out of state. Mark informed me that it wasn't "right" for my boss to replace me in this manner, but that he was sick and tired of the situation my job was imposing on our

THE HAND *of the* HOLY SPIRIT

lives. He told me not to fight this job loss. As a result, I told my boss whatever he wanted to do was fine with me. Mark and I had decided when we moved to Michigan that we were going to purchase a house that would allow us to survive on a single income. We honestly felt it was okay if I went without a job for a period of time, so I relaxed in the situation my boss was imposing on my life.

I continued to look for jobs in Michigan and finally received an offer. There was a position that was available on exactly the same day that my replacement was scheduled to start work in Cincinnati! Isn't it wonderful the way God works in our lives? I have complete faith that God had everything under control during this difficult time in our lives. It's too coincidental that the job in Michigan became available on the exact date that I was going to lose my position in Cincinnati. God, once again, showed how awesome he is and how well he cares for his children. In addition I was being hired into a higher-level position in Michigan. God not only brought me to Michigan, but he made sure I was brought back at the same level I had held before things got really bad with my boss!

Isaiah 42:8-9 says, "I am the Lord; that is my name! I will not give my glory to another or my praise to idols. See, the former things have taken place, and new things I declare; before they spring into being I announce them to you."

This scripture is perfect because God had so many things under control in our lives during this time frame. He guided Mark and me through this time in our lives and moved us into a perfect situation. He saw everything and made sure everything worked out to our benefit. He permitted me to endure some difficult times at work so that I would have plenty of vacation time saved to allow me to search for a new job and hunt for a new home in Michigan. God knew the

Norwood Assembly Plant was not a good location for Mark and guided him to the Orion Assembly Plant, an assembly plant in which he had made sure there were people who could help Mark obtain a job. God even made sure the assembly plant had a floor that would make it easier for Mark's legs. God handled everything perfectly at this time in our lives.

I informed my boss that I had found another position in Michigan and that I would be using my remaining vacation to look for homes. Mark and I both looked very hard for a new home but there just didn't seem to be anything in our price range. We decided that we didn't want to buy a house that was more expensive due to our previous financial situation. We were both getting a little discouraged but I continued to pray about the situation. I knew that I wanted to be placed wherever God wanted me to be, so I prayed diligently while searching for a new home in Michigan. It finally reached a point where I had used virtually all of my vacation time looking for homes. I had just a few days left and Mark and I still hadn't found a home that we were comfortable with. On my last trip to Michigan I told the Lord that I absolutely had to find a home on this trip to Michigan. I told him that I didn't have any more vacation days left and that I needed to find a home. I told him that I had complete trust in him and that I wanted to live where he placed me. I also asked him for a sign so that I would recognize the house he had chosen for us as soon as I saw it.

Mark knew I had been praying about the situation and he told me he had no doubt my prayer would be answered. That day Mark called me from work. He informed me that someone he worked with had told him about a house that had been on the market for over a year. We set up an appointment to go through the house. Amazingly, when we pulled up to the house it had a huge real estate sign in the front yard that read "Partridge." Normally that wouldn't be a big deal, but "Partridge" is my maiden name. I took this as a sign from God that this was the place he had prepared for us in Michigan. The house was beautiful. It had a lot of land and many acres of vacant land across the street. Mark and I both came to know our neighbors and dearly loved them. They had a son who was the same age as Tami and Tom. He was a great friend to them and had strong morals. He made the transition into the new school system a lot easier for Tami and Tom.

The home was also located in the Lake Orion School District. Mark and I felt that this school district offered a well-rounded education for Tami and Tom. Lake Orion had a strong academic standing and was well rounded in all of its extracurricular activities. Mark and I had placed Lake Orion at the top of our list early in our home search. We also had some credit problems during this time in our lives. We had co-signed for a loan that was now in default. As a result of co-signing for this loan our credit had been damaged. Mark and I worried that our damaged credit might affect our ability to purchase a home in Michigan. It turned out that this house was available on a land contract, so we didn't even need to worry about any credit checks! We purchased the home for exactly the amount of money we were comfortable paying. We lived in the house for many years and dearly loved the neighbors, the school system, and the area. Tom loved all of the vacant land across the street and both Tami and Tom formed great relationships with our neighbors' son.

God taught me a lot during these difficult times in my life. He taught me to save money and live below my means. He taught me to have compassion for people who couldn't find work and didn't know how they were going to pay their bills. He taught me to be patient in difficult situations. He taught me that he has everything well under his control at all times in my life, and that I may be required to endure tough times for the best ultimate result.

Soon after we moved to Michigan both the Norwood Assembly Plant and the Oldsmobile Zone Office, where I had been employed, closed. Coworkers I knew in my previous position were now facing layoffs. I never harbored any ill feelings toward any of the people I worked with in Cincinnati. The scriptures teach us not to be vengeful and not to hold grudges against anyone. The Bible teaches us that vengeance is the Lord's.

Proverbs 26:27 (NLT) says, "If you set a trap for others, you will get caught in it yourself, if you roll a boulder down on others, it will roll back and crush you."

Proverbs 20:22 (NLT) says, "Don't say, 'I will get even for this wrong.' Wait for the Lord to handle the matter."

It's interesting that Mark was given the insight to know that the Norwood Assembly Plant was going to be shut down shortly. As for me, I had no idea that there were plans to close the Oldsmobile Zone Office in Cincinnati. Had we stayed in Cincinnati, Mark and I would have both been without jobs. We got out of Cincinnati at exactly the right time. In addition, God provided a geographic location that was only a few hours from Cincinnati. This enabled us to make short trips to Cincinnati whenever our relatives needed us. I believe the Holy Spirit was directing our lives during this time. If he hadn't been watching out for our family we might have become stranded in Cincinnati with no income for our family.

TOM'S ATV ACCIDENT

Soon after we moved to Michigan, Tom found several friends who had dirt bikes and ATVs. Tom immediately fell in love with riding dirt bikes. One night, when Tom was about fourteen or fifteen, Mark bought him a new ATV. Some of his friends already had four-wheelers and Tom had mentioned how "cool" they were. Tom had been doing well in school and had been adjusting well to the move to Michigan, so Mark decided that Tom should have a new four-wheeler. One night after work, Mark brought the new four-wheeler home on the back of a pickup truck. Mark barged into the house, yelling for Tom as if he was angry about something. Tom had no idea what Mark would have been angry about but ran upstairs to meet Mark in the kitchen. Mark looked at Tom and said in a stern voice, "Come outside, I want to show you something!" Tom, of course, was sure he had done something wrong and was in big trouble. Mark took Tom to the back of the pickup truck and said, "I bought something for you." Tom was overjoyed! Mark and Tom unloaded the four-wheeler and Tom took off across the street to try it out.

Our house was situated across the street from state land that had countless riding trails. Tom and his friends spent hours riding their ATVs across the street. Oftentimes they would stay out all night camping and riding their ATVs. We had a few rules about the ATVs. 1) Always ride with a friend. 2) Always wear a helmet. 3) Never ride down the road. I thought we had made all of these rules pretty clear, and I knew that Tom always wore a helmet and road with friends. What I didn't know was that occasionally he would ride his four-wheeler right down the middle of Clarkston Road between two of his friends' houses. Apparently, it was much quicker to ride down the road than it was to ride through the back trails.

One day Tom was at a friend's house. Earlier in the day they had picked up another friend who didn't have a four-wheeler but was one of Tom's best friends. They had become friends during football season — they both played football and shared a locker at school. At some point, they decided to take their friend back home. Tom's friend had decided to ride on the back of the four-wheeler of a mutual friend, so Tom was riding alone. Tom was the lead ATV as they rode down Clarkston Road.

A teenage boy had decided to test-drive a brand new Laser XT from a car dealership. He was traveling at a high rate of speed down Clarkston Road at the same time the boys were riding to Tom's friend's house. Tom looked over his shoulder prior to making a left-hand turn onto his friend's road. He saw a car approaching him from behind, but the car seemed far enough away to allow Tom to complete his turn. Tom must have misjudged the speed of the car because he was struck while completing his turn.

I received a phone call from Tom's friend's mother. She said that a car had hit Tom. She said that the friends had been behind Tom and witnessed the accident. She told me that Tom's friends didn't think that Tom was seriously injured because they saw him stand up after the accident, but they were afraid to remain at the scene of the accident. The boys knew they shouldn't have been on the road with their four-wheelers and were afraid of the police. She said that both of Tom's friends were at her house and that she was going to go to the scene of the accident to find out how bad it was. I was terrified. This was the worst news I could ever imagine. I was horrified to hear that a car had hit Tom. I had no idea how serious the accident was or how badly Tom had been hurt. I knew, however, that many accidents on the road that involved motorcycles or ATVs were fatal and I feared the worst.

Waiting for a second phone call seemed to take a thousand years, but when I got the second call it was a huge relief. Tom's friend's mother said Tom appeared a bit shaken up, but in perfect health. He had some scratches and bruises, but he appeared to have no broken bones or any serious damage. She said that his helmet was cracked from the impact on the asphalt road but he seemed to be coherent and didn't seem to have any head trauma. She said the car that hit Tom had flipped over one and a half times in the air and had landed on its roof more than 100 feet past the place of initial impact. She said the driver of the car had also been walking around and appeared to look unhurt, but the police had ordered the driver to go to a local hospital via ambulance as a precaution. She said it would also be a good idea to have Tom checked out at a hospital and offered to drive him to St. Joseph hospital. She wanted to make sure that he hadn't suffered any head trauma. She was concerned because it was obvious from the cracked helmet that he had taken a severe hit on the road. I was a bit upset that the police had decided that only the driver of the car needed to go to the hospital as a "precautionary" measure. I would have thought that my son would be required to see a doctor, too. After all, who would have had more protection in the accident, a person on an ATV or a person in a car? I was extremely thankful that Tom seemed to be okay and I decided to meet him at the hospital.

When I arrived at the hospital I found that Tom had only minor cuts and bruises. The doctor said that the teenager who had been driving the car had been seen at the hospital and that he was released as well, with minor cuts and bruises. I was thankful that both boys appeared to be fine after the accident. I called Mark and Tom and I decided to go straight from the hospital to the assembly plant. When Mark saw that Tom was fine they both embraced. Tom apologized for riding his four-wheeler on the road but Mark didn't seem to care. The most important thing was that Tom was okay.

I don't believe in chance or luck. I believe the Holy Spirit has a hand in everything that happens to the people who believe in him. Each morning and night I pray that God will keep my family safe from harm and that he will guide each of us through our days. I believe that God answered my prayer and kept Tom safe on this day. I know that God's hand was at work during this accident. Guardian angels were at work to keep everyone safe from injury. The Bible makes it clear that guardian angels are servants to those who believe in Jesus Christ. They watch over us and assist us.

Psalms 34:7-8 (NLT) says, "The angel of the Lord guards all who fear him, and he rescues them. Taste and see that the Lord is good. Oh, the joys of those who trust in him."

Hebrews 1:14 (NLT) says, "Angels are only servants. They are spirits sent from God to care for those who will receive salvation."

I don't believe that it was mere "luck" that Tom was riding alone. Tom has told me that this was not typically the case. He said that most of the time, prior to the accident, his friend rode on the back of Tom's four-wheeler. Having looked at the aftermath of the accident I can tell you that anyone on the back of Tom's four-wheeler would probably have been killed. I was also told that, according to the accident reports, the driver of the car wasn't wearing his seat belt. I don't think it was mere "luck" that the driver was able to sustain one and a half flips in the air, have the car land on its roof over 100 feet from the initial impact site, and walk away from the accident without injury. I also don't think it was "luck" that while riding his ATV Tom sustained being hit by a car traveling at a high rate of speed and walked away without serious injury. I believe that my son, as well as the driver of the car, had guardian angels watching over them, making sure they escaped this accident without serious injury. I know that the Holy Spirit had a hand in making sure that nobody was on the back of Tom's four-wheeler. I know that if my son had a hand in the death of his best friend it would have affected his life forever.

For about two weeks after this accident we could barely get Tom to speak a word. He ran through the scenario of the accident countless times in his mind and knew that the presence of his ATV on Clarkston Road could have cost him his life, his friend's life, and the life of the teenage boy driving the automobile. Had this accident caused serious injury or death to anyone, I know that Tom would probably have been unable to recover from guilt. I thank God that everyone involved in this accident escaped without any injuries.

The TIMELY SELECTION *of a* DOCTOR

I was going through some very stressful circumstances in Michigan. Tami and Tom had both recently graduated from the University of Michigan-Flint and both of them had married shortly after their graduations. I changed jobs within General Motors and was in the process of learning a completely new role. To make matters worse, the drive to work for my new position was too long from our home in Lake Orion. Consequently, I had to move away from neighbors that I had grown to dearly love. I had just moved into Wixom, Michigan, and was still trying to get everything situated in the new house. I didn't know anyone in the new community and was just starting to explore it.

One morning I had an appointment for my annual exam with my gynecologist. The exam went pretty well except that my gynecologist noticed that my blood pressure was elevated quite a bit. I had been seeing her for several years and had never had a problem with high blood pressure before, so this really was unusual for me. When my gynecologist informed me of my elevated blood pressure, I told her that I wasn't concerned about it because I had been going through some very stressful times and I was sure that was the source of the problem. She told me that she was still concerned about the high blood pressure, because she had seen me before when I was under stress and my blood pressure remained normal. We talked about it and she made me promise to keep a close eye on my blood pressure.

She told me that elevated blood pressure can be dangerous and if the problem didn't go away, I needed to have some tests. I told her that I would keep an eye on my blood pressure and left the office thinking everything was okay.

A few months later I became really sick. I was having difficulty breathing and had a lot of congestion. I decided to call my boss and tell him that I wouldn't be able to make it into work that day. Mark wasn't feeling very well either so we both decided that we were going to be seen by a doctor. Having just moved into the Wixom area, I didn't have a local doctor. I decided to start looking for a doctor who was fairly close to the house because I didn't want to drive all the way back to Lake Orion every time I was sick. I based my selection criteria on a few things. First, I wanted a doctor who was an actual medical doctor, not a doctor of osteopathy. In Lake Orion, Mark and I never could find a doctor who was an actual M.D. and this bothered both of us, so we decided that this time we were going to look for an M.D. Second, I wanted a doctor who was close to the house because it was winter in Michigan and this day was very cold and snowy outside. I didn't want to drive that far. Third, I wanted to be seen by an internist. With this set of criteria in mind I decided to pray and ask the Lord to lead me to a good doctor. I told him that a good doctor was so important and I left the matter in God's hands. I pray about every aspect of my life. I very rarely make any major decision without consulting God through prayer. This was no exception. After I said a short prayer I opened the phone book and found a doctor's office that had two M.D.s who fit my criteria. I had to make a decision between which of the two M.D.s to see, so I based this final decision solely on the fact that one of the M.D.s had the first name of Mark. It may sound like a crazy way to select a doctor but I was comfortable with my selection process.

I called the doctor's office and was told that they could see Mark and me right away. They told me to come right over to the office. This concerned Mark a little bit because he always felt that if a doctor was really good, it would be difficult to get an appointment. Mark questioned me about my selection and wondered if these doctors were any good, but I told him that I really needed to see a doctor and these doctors could see us right away. When I arrived at the doctor's office I questioned the nurse at the front desk. I told her that Mark and I were both a little concerned that they were able to see us on such short notice. She informed me that the office was booked solid that day, but that the doctor had informed the nurses not to turn anyone away on this particular day. The doctor told the nurses that the weather conditions were so bad outside that if anyone called for an appointment to get them in. He said anyone who was going to brave the weather to see him on this day must really be sick and needed to see a doctor. Consequently, the nurses were instructed not to turn anyone away. The nurse informed me that, had I called on a different day, the doctor probably wouldn't have seen me. This news made Mark and me feel a little better about the doctor we had selected.

When the doctor examined me he found that my blood pressure was elevated to the point that he questioned me about it and asked me if I had ever had a problem with high blood pressure before. I informed him that I didn't typically have high blood pressure and that this was uncommon for me. He told me that high blood pressure could be dangerous and told me that we would need to keep an eye on it. He said that if it didn't go back to normal that he would need to run some tests in order to figure out what might be causing it. At that point I remembered that my gynecologist had also seen high blood pressure during my annual exam, so I told the doctor that we really needed to figure out what was causing this right away. I asked him to run tests immediately in order to determine what the problem was. He agreed, thinking it was important since my gynecologist was also concerned about my high blood pressure.

The doctor started to ask me several questions. He noticed that my skin appeared very dry and itchy and that my hair was very dry and brittle. He noticed that my nails were breaking and were peeling in layers. He also noticed that my eyelashes had been falling out. He asked me about all of these conditions and I informed him that I wasn't very concerned about them. I told him that my skin was dry and itchy because I had just moved into a new house. I am very allergic to things and I told him that I was sure that I was just getting used to the new water at the house. In addition, I told him that the house had wool carpeting and that I was allergic to wool. As for my hair, I had just had it colored. I figured that this was the reason it was so dry and brittle. I assumed my nails were breaking easily because I am allergic to cleaning agents and I have always had bad nails.

Finally, I attributed my eyelashes falling out to the high level of stress that I was under. The doctor asked me several other questions. He asked me if I had been experiencing any changes in my sleep patterns lately. I said that Mark had told me that I was frightening him at night because I was sleeping so deeply lately. Mark told me that I was sleeping so deeply that they could probably move the house without waking me up. I told the doctor, however, that I really felt this was due to exhaustion. I explained that there were so many major changes occurring in my life that I was having a hard time coping with the stress. Finally the doctor asked if any of my

142

immediate relatives had died at an early age. I told him that both my mother and father had died at an early age. I told him that my mother had died of a sudden heart attack and my father had died of pneumonia.

The doctor completed his examination and told me that he wanted to run some additional tests. He felt that I might have a problem with my thyroid gland. He told me that I had very good excuses for all of the medical conditions, but the collection of all of those conditions pointed to problems with my thyroid that couldn't be ignored. He informed me that he was an expert in diagnosing thyroid problems. He told me that he had written a paper in college about thyroid conditions that went undiagnosed. He said this subject interested him quite a bit and that this could be a very deadly condition. He said many people die of heart attacks as a result of undiagnosed thyroid problems. My mother's death at an early age also pointed to a possible problem with my thyroid since the condition is hereditary. It was his professional opinion that my mother could have had an undiagnosed thyroid condition that contributed to her heart attack.

It turned out that the doctor correctly diagnosed problems with my thyroid at an early stage of the disease. The doctor was able to prescribe medication that corrected the condition. I have suffered some minor problems with my heart as a result of my thyroid condition. The damage that has already been done to my heart cannot be reversed but is treatable with medication. Had this condition gone undiagnosed for much longer, I am certain that I could have died of a heart attack at an early age, just as my mother had. God was responsible for leading me to a perfect doctor. God knew that something was seriously wrong with me and that I needed help.

Psalms 32:7 (NLT) says, "You are my hiding place; you will protect me from trouble and surround me with songs of deliverance."

It turned out that God led me to a doctor who was an expert in diagnosing the very condition that was creating a problem. I had no idea that I was seriously ill. God knew that I needed help and he made sure that I got the help when I needed it. God truly does look after his chosen people.

BOUND *by*
IRRATIONAL
FEARS

I was always an extremely fearful person. In fact, my mother didn't go back to work on a full-time basis after I started school because I used to come home from school and frantically search for her if she wasn't there. If I couldn't find her right away I would oftentimes panic and start screaming and yelling for her. I was so timid that I would never go anywhere on my own. In fact, I don't remember ever going out on my own until I was about eighteen years old. If there wasn't someone to go with me I simply didn't go because I was too timid and afraid. In addition, my first marriage was very abusive. My husband was a diagnosed schizophrenic and could become a very violent person. The violence got so bad in our relationship that I finally had no choice but to divorce him. As a result of all of this violence in my life I became bound by the fear of interacting with other people.

Mark and I were involved in a terrible car accident in 1985. We were on vacation in Kentucky and were waiting in a line of stopped traffic. The traffic was waiting to make a left-hand turn into Churchill Downs Racetrack. I was seated in the backseat of our car. We were going to the racetrack with some very good friends when a man ran into the back of our car at a high rate of speed. Apparently, he was eating McDonald's food and failed to pay attention to the road. I

145

endured months of physical therapy as a result of the car accident and I have never fully recovered.

I still have problems with my back to this day. Because of the accident I became extremely fearful of driving a car or riding in a car. Consequently, I was not only afraid of socializing with people, but I had a difficult time getting into a car. These fears almost completely bound me to my house.

I found it very difficult to face my fear and walk out the front door every morning for work. I knew, however, that God didn't place Christians on earth to have a spirit of fear. I knew that I would be sinning against God if I didn't socialize with other people and try to lead them toward a relationship with him. I sought psychiatric care for my fear because I needed someone to help explain to me how the mind worked and what was causing this irrational fear. I found the psychiatric sessions to be very useful, but I could never seem to get past my fear. My psychiatrist told me that the only way to get past my fear would be to confront it. He said if I really wanted to get past my fear I needed to get to a point in my life where I could remain in a room with a lot of commotion and not leave that environment. He said if I could do this I would be confronting my fear and on the road to long-term recovery. I, however, had a very difficult time doing this and I continued to be bound by fear. Finally, at one of our sessions my psychiatrist told me that I needed to make a choice. He said I had two options: I could either remain in my home the rest of my life, where I was comfortable, or I could socialize with other people and take the risk that they might hurt me. His statements forced me to re-evaluate the way I was thinking.

Prior to this point I thought that a psychiatrist was the only person who could help me through my fear. His statement, more or less, made me realize that the decision to get over my fear was really my own decision. I had been praying about my fear for many years but I finally decided that it was time to turn all of my fear over to God and give it to him through prayer. I told God that I was an extremely fearful person, but that I knew he didn't want me to shut myself up in my house. I told him that I felt I would be committing a sin against him if I locked myself in my house, and I asked him to help me overcome my fear so that I wouldn't sin against him. At that moment a scripture entered my mind. Mathew 8:23-27 says the following:

> *Then he got into the boat and his disciples followed him. Without warning, a furious storm came up on the lake, so that the waves swept over the boat. But Jesus was sleeping. The disciples went and woke him, saying, "Lord, save us! We're going to drown!" He replied, "You of little faith, why are you so afraid?" Then he got up and rebuked the winds and the waves, and it was completely calm. The men were amazed and asked, "What kind of man is this? Even the winds and the waves obey him!"*

I began to equate my fear with the way Jesus calmed the storm on the lake. I asked God to help me deal with my fear. I have come to realize that God will protect me from harm. I know that he loves and cares for his followers. I know that even if someone does hurt me it would be because he permitted the harm to come to me. That would be okay because I would still be accomplishing God's will. This realization has liberated me from the irrational fears that were binding me. I'm still not totally comfortable socializing with people or driving in an automobile, but I have found that I can face my fear with the knowledge that I have God looking after me. Nothing will ever happen to me that he doesn't permit. This realization has enabled me to function despite the binding fears that I face everyday. I have learned that the perfect love of the Holy Spirit can overcome my irrational fears.

2 Corinthians 3:17 says, "Now, the Lord is the Spirit, and wherever the Spirit of the Lord is, he gives freedom."

This verse is so true. It is the spirit of the Lord that has given me freedom from the irrational fears that bound me for so many years. I still struggle with my fear at times, but I don't permit it to rule my life. The knowledge that nothing will ever happen to me that the Holy Spirit doesn't permit has given me freedom from my irrational fears that otherwise would have bound me to my house.

PRAYERS
for DEBBIE

During one of our Sunday morning services the pastor of our church challenged everyone to select a few people in their lives and pray for them each and every day for seven weeks. He told us not to let the people know that we would be praying for them and asked us to watch how our prayers enabled God to work in their lives. Mark and I took this challenge very seriously because we had seen how effective the power of prayer had been in our lives. We talked about whom to pray for and decided that we were going to pray for someone very close to us who didn't seem to have a very consistent relationship with Jesus. Mark and I decided to pray for my cousin Debbie. She was going through some difficult times in her life. Separated from her husband, a man she dearly loved, Debbie called me several times and told me how lonely she was. Her mother had also passed away and she was having a difficult time coming to grips with the death of her mother. She also told me that she was having a difficult time making friends and didn't have anyone to turn to. Debbie had grown up in Cincinnati but had moved to Wisconsin a few years prior to her separation from her husband. As a result, she felt isolated and alone following her separation. I prayed that God would provide Debbie with some companions in Wisconsin and that he would soften her heart so she would truly become a born-again Christian and have a personal relationship with her heavenly Father.

Debbie had been raised in the Catholic Church. She had prayed to St. Jude on my behalf at a young age and I attribute my pregnancy with the twins to her prayers. She was in and out of church but didn't seem to have a solid and consistent relationship with her heavenly Father. Mark and I both dearly loved Debbie and felt she needed to be lifted up through prayer so we decided to make her one of the primary targets of our prayers. We prayed for Debbie each and every day for well over seven weeks. We didn't have the opportunity to witness how God was working in her life because she lived so far away. This didn't give us much of an opportunity to see each other and we didn't talk over the phone that often. Mark and I felt certain, however, that God would answer our prayers and work in her life.

One day, several months after Mark and I had started praying, I got a call from her. Debbie sounded so excited! She asked me, "Pam, do you know that there really is a God?"

I answered, "Yes, I know there is."

She responded, "No, I mean do you know that there REALLY is a God that looks out for you and listens to your prayers and wants to have a relationship with you?"

I answered again, "Yes, Debbie, I have known this for years, but what makes you so certain that there is a God?"

Debbie told me that after the death of her mother she questioned herself about many things in her life. She started wondering about her spiritual life and how she could be sure about her salvation. She explained that one Sunday, running late for mass, she decided to attend a new Catholic church. She liked the priest and decided to start attending this new church. She had become good friends with some Catholic ladies at the church.

She explained that the ladies took her into their group almost as soon as she started attending the church. She felt comfortable with them. As a matter of fact, they prayed together as a group at the church every morning at 6:00 a.m. Debbie also told me that she quit her job so that she could explore a closer relationship with her heavenly Father. She said she was working in a nursing home and was even giving out communion to some of the people in the nursing home. One story really struck me. Debbie told me that she and the ladies traveled to Majagoria, Bosnia-Herzogovina, formerly part of communist Yugoslavia, and famous for sightings of the Virgin Mary. Debbie said there are numerous accounts of miracles that have occurred in this Croatian region of Europe. She told me that, prior to going to Majagoria, she was very skeptical of the stories of the miracles but she decided she needed to find out for herself if they were true or not.

She said she decided to make the trip with the ladies as a skeptic, but the stories were too intriguing to ignore. Debbie enjoyed her trip to Majagoria; the people were extremely poor but they were incredibly humble and gracious hosts. She said there weren't any hotels in this part of Croatia, so they had to stay in local homes. Debbie said she was amazed at what she saw. She said she witnessed numerous amazing healings. In addition, Debbie said the region surrounding this small community was involved in a terrible war, but this community had never been seriously hit by mortar shells or bombs. She heard that the priests prayed constantly during the war and she felt that God had placed his hand over the community to spare it from the ravages of war.

While she was in Majagoria, Debbie made a pilgrimage to a Catholic church. This church was situated on top of a hill that many Catholics visited each year. While praying at the alter she was touched directly by the Holy Spirit. The charismatic Catholics had a specific term for her experience. They called it being "slain" in the Spirit. I'm not exactly sure what that term means but, the way Debbie described it, she was touched by the Holy Spirit as she was praying. She became unconscious and was laid in a position on her back. The priests said that the entire time she was in this position she continued to pray audibly even though she was clearly unconscious. Soon after Debbie regained consciousness the priest of the church told her that he had never seen anyone take so completely to the Holy Spirit. He told her that someone must have been praying for her and God must have prepared her heart for salvation because she took so quickly and completely to the Holy Spirit.

Debbie continued her relationship with these charismatic Catholic ladies. She became very good friends with the priest in Majagoria who had witnessed her baptism in the Spirit. She visited the area of Majagoria on numerous other occasions and never doubted that miracles were occurring in that area of the world. She had no doubt that God was at work in Majagoria and within her life. Mark and I had been praying for Debbie's conversion for several months prior to this phone call.

I had also been praying that God would provide companionship for Debbie in Wisconsin. I have no doubt that God answered our prayers and worked within Debbie's life during this difficult period of time.

PAULA'S CANCER

My sister Paula was diagnosed with skin cancer in the winter of 2001. When she finally had the cancer diagnosed it was too late for the doctors to treat it effectively. The doctors tried to treat the illness but Paula's prognosis wasn't good. By June of 2002 the cancer had progressed and spread throughout her body. Paula was living in Tennessee at the time and I made several trips to Tennessee in order to help her through her illness. The trip I made to Tennessee in June of 2002 was much different than any trip I had taken previously. I received a phone call from Paula's husband that she had taken a turn for the worse. She was bleeding internally and the doctors didn't think she had much longer to live. The doctors assumed that her bleeding was a result of the advanced stages of cancer. They had already stopped actively treating Paula for cancer and, at this point, were only managing her pain through drug therapy. She was taken completely off cancer medications and she did not want to be resuscitated if she died. The doctors thought, at most, Paula had two weeks to live.

I prayed for Paula every night after I found out about her illness. Paula had been a dedicated church worker for much of her life, but had kind of walked away from God. I had real doubts about her salvation and I prayed that she would reaffirm her faith in Jesus before she died. Mark and I also contacted our pastor about this situation. I told him that on my previous trips to visit with Paula I had been unable to make her realize how dire her situation was.

I couldn't make her understand that she could die of this disease and that her salvation was extremely important. No matter how hard I tried to bring up the subject of salvation she didn't want to talk about it. The pastor said he would pray about this situation and told me that many times the best way to witness to a person is to tell them how God has worked within your own life.

That night, as I made the trip down to Tennessee, I prayed that the Lord would provide me an opportunity to witness to my sister so that she might commit her life to Jesus. I also prayed for a sign from Jesus that if Paula committed her life to Christ I would know for sure that her salvation was assured. I had many concerns. The doctor had told Paula's husband that Paula might not make it through the night. In addition, she was on heavy pain medication and most of the time she was unable to carry on a coherent conversation. I wasn't sure that I would be able to carry on a normal conversation with her, much less witness to her. I also prayed for safe travel to Tennessee because I was making the trip by myself. Mark had to work and couldn't take time off on such short notice, so I had no traveling companion.

The trip through the night to Tennessee was fairly uneventful. I arrived at the hospital and found that my sister was in pretty bad condition. She had painful open sores all over her body and face. The doctors had placed her on extremely heavy pain medication. This helped control the pain but it also made it very difficult to talk with her. The medication caused her to hallucinate and become extremely paranoid.

Paula had an extreme fear of insects and she was terrified by the small holes in the wall of her hospital room. I spent much of my time placing bandages over small holes in the wall because she thought they were bugs. In addition, Paula had become very frightened about her condition. She was extremely bitter toward her husband and caregivers. She had episodes of screaming and had a difficult time grasping that there were other patients around her who were also very sick and needed rest.

Growing up with Paula afforded me the experience of knowing that this was how she typically reacted when she was afraid. Instead of showing her fear she would lash out at anyone close to her. I wanted to talk with her in order to find out what she was most afraid about, but I initially found it difficult to talk to her because of the heavy doses of pain medication. That night I decided to stay at the hospital with Paula. I wanted to give her husband a break for a while and I also wanted to have some time alone with my sister. I sat by her bedside, constantly praying for her and asking God to provide an opportunity for me to witness to her. My prayers were answered during that night in the hospital. Paula started to get belligerent with her caregivers again. I knew that there were other extremely sick people in the hospital and I told Paula that her fits of anger weren't fair to the other people around her. At that moment I asked Paula what she was most afraid of. Paula broke down. She began to cry and told me that she was very afraid of death and was unsure of her salvation. I knew that this was an answer to my prayer and an opportunity to witness. Paula told me that she trusted me and wanted me to tell her if I thought she was going to die.

She didn't trust her doctors to give her an honest answer. I told Paula that I didn't know if she was going to die or not, that this was in God's hands. I told her that I hoped and prayed that she wouldn't die but that things didn't look good for her. Again, at this point Paula told me that she was afraid of dying.

I asked Paula why she was so afraid of death and I asked her about her salvation. I told Paula that I was sure of my salvation and asked her if she, too, wanted to be sure of her salvation. Paula broke down and started to cry. She said that she wanted to be sure of her salvation and asked me to pray for her. I asked Paula if she remembered what she had been taught about salvation and asked her if she wanted to commit her life to Jesus. Paula said she wanted to commit her life to Jesus but didn't know how to pray for that. I helped Paula pray for her salvation that night in the hospital.

We prayed together and I felt the presence of God. As soon as I noticed the feeling, Paula asked me to sit her up in bed. At first I thought Paula might be having another panic attack but she told me that she felt the presence of the Holy Spirit and wanted to sit up in bed. We both felt his presence that night in the hospital room. I sat Paula up in bed and she poured her soul out to the Holy Spirit. She prayed for forgiveness for every past sin in her life. Her prayer was one of the most awesome experiences I have had as a Christian! After witnessing Paula's prayer for salvation I felt much more at ease about her salvation. I felt at peace because the Lord had given me a sign that he had heard my sister's prayers. I felt that I could now travel back to Michigan with the peace of mind that my sister had been granted salvation.

The next morning my sister's prognosis improved. Her internal bleeding was under control and the doctors expected her to live a while longer. I decided to make the trip back to Michigan because I was sure there would be future trips to Tennessee. I believed that my sister's immediate danger had passed. The trip back to Michigan was extremely tiring but peaceful. I couldn't wait to tell Mark about the wonderful experience that Paula and I had shared in Tennessee that night in her hospital room. I was finally sure that my sister's salvation was assured and that the blood of Jesus Christ had washed away all of her past transgressions.

A few days later I received a phone call from Paula's husband. He said the open sores on Paula's face seemed to be disappearing. He said Paula's sores just seemed to be "drying up." The doctors were baffled. They told him that they had never seen anything like this before. Paula's skin cancer seemed to be simply going away on its own. There were no documented cases in medical history of skin cancer in such an advanced stage simply going away on its own. To make matters even more inexplicable, doctors had previously taken Paula off all cancer medications. Her cancer had become so advanced that it was deemed to be incurable and the doctors were only managing Paula's pain. The doctors could not understand why the cancer would be healing, but thought it might be a result of some chemical reaction. As a result, they decided that they weren't going to modify Paula's drug regimen even though it didn't include any medication that would have been combating the cancer in Paula's body. The doctors wanted to perform some tests to see if the same thing was happening on the inside of her body but Paula was too weak for them to conduct any internal tests.

Paula's husband said that Paula's outlook and demeanor changed after the night I spent with her in the hospital. She was no longer as paranoid or afraid and she wasn't lashing out at her caregivers any longer. I believe this sudden change of personality can be explained only through the great peace we receive when we become saved and truly commit our lives to Jesus. Jesus washes away our sins and completely transforms us. Paula's personality changed in one night. God provided the peace she had been longing for and Paula was no longer afraid of death.

I prayed for three things during the drive to Tennessee. I prayed for safe travel, an opportunity to witness to my sister, and a sign that my sister's salvation was secure. I know that my prayers were answered that night. God knew how important it was for me to have an opportunity to witness to my sister, and he knew how important it was for me to be assured of my sister's salvation. He has fulfilled both of those answers to prayer in a magnificent manner. He is an awesome and loving God.

A little while after returning to Michigan I received a phone call from Tennessee. I was told that my sister was probably going to die very soon. The doctors found two more inoperable tumors on Paula's spine. I continued to pray that God would take my sister with as little pain as possible when she died. I am much more at peace with my sister's death now that I know her salvation is secure. The sores on Paula's face had completely healed. They left no scars behind. It's fitting that the sores on Paula's face completely healed just as all of her past transgressions have been completely washed clean through the blood of Jesus Christ! What a miraculous and fitting sign the Holy Spirit has chosen to provide for me that he has answered my sister's plea for salvation! While I still prayed that my sister would recover and that God would completely heal her, I knew that this decision was in God's hands. I thanked God, saying that if he decided to take my sister home to heaven she would look beautiful in her casket. Her face was no longer scarred and disfigured by the cancer. God's healing hand had restored her beauty and restored her spirit.

A few weeks later I received another phone call. My sister Paula had passed away. The funeral was held in Cincinnati, where most of Paula's family lives. Mark and I traveled to Cincinnati to attend the funeral together. It was extremely difficult to say good-bye to my sister, but the peace of mind knowing that we will see each other again in heaven made attending the funeral a much more bearable experience. I thank God for his answers to prayers. I don't know how I would have been able to bear this funeral without the knowledge that my sister's salvation was secure.

D E B B I E ' S
D E A T H

When Paula was diagnosed with cancer I decided to make the trip to Tennessee for her surgery. I received a phone call from Debbie late one night. I had left a message for her regarding Paula's condition, but had been unable to get in contact with her. Debbie had just returned from Majagoria. She apologized for calling me so late but wanted some information so she could pray for Paula. I gave the information to Debbie and she decided she was going to fly to Cincinnati so that we could meet there and make the drive together to Tennessee. My sister Jackie was also going to Tennessee, and we all decided to stay in Paula's house with her husband because we didn't have a lot of money for a hotel.

I was really thankful that Debbie had decided to make the trip to Tennessee because it gave us an opportunity to talk about all of the things that were going on in her life. She had completely committed her life to serving Jesus. She had made several trips to Majagoria and had been working in a nursing home where she gave communion. In addition, she had become very close friends with a lady from her Catholic church. I loved to hear all of Debbie's experiences and I loved to take the opportunity to pray with Debbie. When we prayed it was like we were two kindred spirits. We could both really feel the power of prayer when praying together. When Debbie and I first arrived in Tennessee we prayed quite a bit for Paula. Paula had a stroke during her surgery and the doctors didn't know if she would recover.

We knew the situation was very serious. In fact, I called everyone in the family to make sure they were aware of the fact that Paula might not live that much longer.

Neither Debbie nor I felt that Paula was spiritually ready to die and we prayed for God to give her a little more time here on earth so that we would have the opportunity to talk with her and witness to her. We wanted Paula to be absolutely assured of her salvation before she died. Paula did manage to recover from the stroke, a real answer to our prayers!

While we were staying at Paula's house, Debbie took it upon herself to snoop around a little bit. Debbie found some things in the house that alarmed me quite a bit. She found a Ouija board as well as several magazines about witchcraft and sorcery. She also found a deck of Tarot cards and some other things that looked like they might be associated with the occult. Apparently, Paula had continued to be intrigued with the thought that she had a gift of prophecy. She had also been working with a lady so that she might hone her skills of prophecy. Apparently, this lady worked with the police to help solve some of their murder cases. The lady had the ability to use her "spiritual powers" to help solve some of these crimes. She believed that the "spiritual powers" were gifts from God. I believe she may have even been a deacon in her church, although I'm not sure what type of church she attended. I was really nervous about these "spiritual powers." The Bible teaches us that we can recognize prophets from God because they will never be wrong. I really didn't think she was a prophet sent from God. In addition, the Bible warns against getting involved with the occult, witchcraft, and sorcery.

It was obvious from the materials that Debbie found in the house that Paula seemed to be involved in, or at least intrigued by, witchcraft and sorcery. This deeply concerned Debbie and me and we prayed about this situation quite a bit.

While we were visiting Paula in the hospital I spent quite a bit of time in the hospital chapel. I remember one incident when I returned from praying that I saw Debbie talking with a man. The man was obviously a patient in the hospital. He was in the standard hospital gown and had an I.V. After they finished talking I asked Debbie what the conversation was all about. Debbie told me that she had noticed this man walking in the hall. She said the man looked really frightened so she approached him and talked with him in order to comfort him. The man said that he was frightened because he was about to have serious back surgery. Debbie took the opportunity to talk with him and prayed for him.

She witnessed to him about how Jesus had worked in her life. She really comforted the man. I loved Debbie; she had been so completely converted by Jesus that she had no problem approaching anyone and witnessing about how Jesus was working in her life. She took every opportunity to witness to people. Debbie, Jackie, and I continued to pray for Paula while we were in Tennessee. Paula made it through her surgery and recovered from her stroke. When her condition started to improve, we left Tennessee.

The day after Debbie prayed for the gentleman in the hospital, I had an odd conversation with her. She said, "You know, Pam, I really need to be careful about who I choose to pray for. You know that man I prayed for yesterday? Well, I really think that when I pray for people, I can sometimes feel their pain. Ever since I prayed for him, the tip of my tongue has been numb."

I thought this was pretty disturbing. Debbie had told me before that after praying for people she had terrible headaches. She had always attributed these headaches and feelings to the fact that she empathized with their pain. She believed she could feel the pain of others through her prayers.

I can't remember what I told Debbie about this but we returned home and I didn't think about it again until I got a phone call from her a few days later. She told me that she had been diagnosed with brain cancer. Apparently, the numbness in her tongue never went away so she had some tests run. The tests revealed that she had inoperable brain cancer and that the cancer had also spread to her lungs. The doctors didn't give her very long to live. In fact they said they would be surprised if she lasted six months.

This was terrible news for me because I loved Debbie. Now I was faced with Debbie dying of cancer in Wisconsin and Paula dying of cancer in Tennessee. This was a dreadful period in my life. The news hit me hard and I visited Debbie several times in Wisconsin. Jackie and I made the trips together several times to Wisconsin to be with Debbie, and to Tennessee to be with Paula. We had decided that as long as we made the trips together we could drive straight through Chicago. I made Jackie promise me, however, that she would never drive straight through Chicago if I wasn't with her. We both believed it was much too dangerous to drive through Chicago alone. The bypass around Chicago was longer but much safer.

I remember the last trip that Jackie and I made together to Wisconsin. We were visiting Debbie in the nursing home. Debbie had been admitted to the nursing home where she used to work. It was a beautiful nursing home and they just happened to have an opening available when she was diagnosed with cancer. It was a true blessing because all of the caregivers knew Debbie and loved her. They had the opportunity to work with her before she became sick so they knew what a sweet and caring lady she was. They really provided and cared for her throughout her stay at the nursing home. During this last trip, Jackie and I could see that Debbie

THE HAND *of the* HOLY SPIRIT

was extremely weak. She had a difficult time sitting up in bed. She was so weak that she couldn't even lift the telephone receiver. Debbie was at peace, though, and she wasn't in that much pain. She said that her body just ached as if she had a bad flu. She told us that she was ready to die because she knew she would be going to be with God. She said that she had prayed for a complete healing but that she was now at peace with her salvation; if God decided not to heal her, it was his decision. She knew God had everything under control.

Things were really difficult for everyone in Debbie's family. She was so young, and her disease was so unexpected that it was difficult for her husband and children to bear. I had some understanding of what everyone must have been going through because I had lost both my father and mother when they were young. It was really hard on the entire family. I was concerned because I wanted to be there for Debbie but I didn't want to intrude on the family. I thought it was important that the family have quality time together before she passed away. I also felt, however, that Debbie wanted me to be with her because we had so much in common. I knew that Debbie loved to pray with me and believed that she could talk with me about all of her most recent religious experiences. I prayed quite a bit about this because I didn't want to intrude on the family but I thought I needed to be there for Debbie.

When it came time for Jackie and me to leave the hospital I got really confused. Debbie and I had talked the night before. I told her that Jackie and I were going to be leaving the next day and that the next time we would see each other again would likely be in heaven. Debbie seemed at peace with this during that night in the hospital. When Jackie and I said our final good-bye to her, however, she thought I was going home to Michigan to get some more clothes but that I would be coming right back up to visit with her again. I didn't know if Debbie wanted me to come back to Wisconsin again, or if the medication was just making her confused, so I didn't know what to do.

Jackie and I returned home and I prayed for several days for the wisdom to know what I should do. I tried calling Debbie's daughter several times but never received an answer so I assumed the family wanted some time alone before she passed away. I didn't want to burden the family so I decided not to travel back to Wisconsin. A few days later I got a call from Debbie's daughter. She told me that Debbie had asked her to call me to say she wanted me to come back to Wisconsin to be with her. I knew this was an answer to my prayer. I had no doubt that God was telling me I needed to be with Debbie, so I packed a few things and got back in the car. This time I was making the trip on my own. Mark couldn't make the trip with me because he had to work and couldn't take time off on such short notice.

During my drive to Wisconsin I prayed about a few things. I didn't want to be a burden on the family but I also didn't like eating alone in restaurants. I told God that I needed to be in Wisconsin with Debbie but that I hated making the trip on my own and I didn't enjoy eating by myself. I asked God for safe travel because I realized that it was dangerous to travel alone. I didn't want to be stranded on the road somewhere all by myself. Debbie had insisted that I stay in her condominium. I was really grateful because I didn't have a lot of money and it would have been difficult for me to pay for a hotel room. When I arrived at the nursing home, Debbie's daughter was sitting with Debbie. Debbie was in pretty good spirits, as she always seemed to be. When it came close to dinnertime, her daughter told me that she was going out to eat with some of her friends. She told me that she didn't have any idea why she had ordered so much food for lunch but that she had quite a bit left over. She told me that it was a Chinese rice dish and that it was really good. She said there was no way she was going to eat it and offered it to me. Of course, I accepted the lunch because I was dreading eating by myself.

The Chinese dish was wonderful and I thanked her (and God) for providing the meal so that I could eat in the hospital room with Debbie that night. Debbie and I talked quite a bit in the hospital room. We really had a wonderful time together. The following night I was with Debbie in the nursing home. She was having a difficult time because the medication was making her nauseous. She couldn't seem to eat anything.

I thought that the medication was causing her nausea and I knew that food oftentimes dilutes the effects of medication. I asked her if anything sounded like it would be good for her to eat. At first she told me that she couldn't think of anything that she wanted to eat. After a while of talking with her, however, she decided that she really was in the mood for a dish that a lady used to make for her. She called the dish "egg strata." I told Debbie that we should call the lady and ask her if she would make some for her. Debbie, of course, thought this was totally out of the question. She didn't want to impose upon the lady. I finally convinced Debbie that people love to do things for people who are in need. I asked Debbie if she had ever done anything for the lady and Debbie said that they were good friends. She had oftentimes done things for her. I finally convinced Debbie that we should call the lady and ask her to make some "egg strata."

I talked to the lady on the phone and she was wonderful. She was excited that she could do something for Debbie. The lady happily agreed to make the dish and even brought it to the hospital. She had made more than enough for both

Debbie and me. It was a wonderful meal. Debbie ate quite a bit and started to feel much better. Again, I thanked the lady (and God) because they had provided another opportunity for me to eat with Debbie in the hospital room. I, once again, didn't need to eat by myself. In fact, I never had to eat alone in a restaurant the entire time I was in Wisconsin. Sometimes God works in funny ways. He knew that I didn't like to eat by myself and he worked it out so that I wouldn't need to worry about it.

Debbie and I had a wonderful time together. This was my final trip to be with Debbie before she passed away. We talked about her spiritual life and all the trips she had made to Majagoria. We talked about how much she loved her husband and children. It was extremely evident that there was quite a bit of love in their family. I really felt at peace when I left the nursing home and headed back to Michigan. I felt that I had been there for Debbie and that I didn't need to worry any longer about what Debbie wanted or needed.

On my way back to Michigan I decided to travel straight through Chicago. I was really homesick and going straight through Chicago was much faster than taking the bypass. I made it safely through Chicago, but when I got home my car was making a terrible noise. Mark found that the serpentine belt had almost completely broken in two. The belt was terribly frayed. He said it was a miracle that I made the trip safely home that night. He told me that I could have very easily been stranded on the road if the serpentine belt had broken. I have no doubt that God protected me and looked out for me while I was traveling home from Wisconsin. It wasn't the smartest thing in the world to drive straight through Chicago, but I knew God had his hand on me and protected me so that I made it home safely from Wisconsin.

Debbie died soon after I returned to Michigan. I wasn't present at her death but I have been told she never experienced much pain. I was told that she never stopped witnessing to people about how God had worked in her life up until the day she died. I have no doubt that Debbie had a complete conversion in Majagoria. The experience she had in that church in Majagoria completely changed her life. I have no doubt that she was a born-again Christian and was called home to be with God in heaven.

MY EARLY RETIREMENT *from* GENERAL MOTORS

Mark took an early retirement from General Motors in 1992. He was experiencing some health problems and we agreed it was best for him to leave his position. His job had become increasingly stressful and he had experienced a mild heart attack earlier that same year. Mark had always worked the night shift and I had always worked the day shift. As a result, we never saw each other that much except on weekends. Mark and I decided that it was time to start seeing each other on a more regular basis, so Mark accepted an early retirement as soon as General Motors made the opportunity available to him. I continued to work for General Motors, however, because I thought we needed my income in order to help make ends meet. Mark had taken another job as a bus driver, which allowed him to work during the day and earn some extra spending money. The job was much less stressful and gave him the opportunity to get out of the house while I was at work. He really enjoyed driving the school bus and talking with the other bus drivers in the garage.

Not too long after Mark retired I also began thinking about retiring from General Motors. I struggled with this because General Motors had always provided a great income.

I became accustomed to a lifestyle where I could buy most anything I wanted. I enjoyed the fact that I never had to worry too much about money. I tend to have fairly expensive taste, especially when it comes to my wardrobe.

I had no problem with this while I was earning an income that enabled me to afford a nice wardrobe, but I knew I wouldn't be able to buy everything I wanted if I retired from General Motors. In addition, I collect Longaberger baskets. They can be expensive, but with the income I was earning from General Motors, I never felt guilty about buying the baskets.

My job was becoming increasingly hectic and was stressful. I had always worked for top executives at General Motors. These executives had very busy lives and I was finding that, with the advancements that had been made in technology, my bosses could now work around the clock. They had laptop computers, cellular phones, and various other tools that permitted them to work at any time of the day and in any geographic location. Since I supported them, I was finding that my job responsibilities were getting more and more demanding. I was having a difficult time keeping up with my spiritual life. It seemed that I was so tired from work that I wasn't having enough time to pray properly. In addition, I wasn't able to attend Wednesday night church services on a regular basis because I was taking work home and completing it when I would have much rather been at church. I also felt guilty because I never seemed to have enough time to help Tami or Tom when they needed me. I never seemed able to watch their children when they got sick. I didn't seem to ever have the time to do the things that I felt a nurturing mother and grandmother should do. My job had become so hectic that I knew it was impeding my ability to be the type of Christian, mother, and grandmother that I wanted to be.

I prayed about the situation and asked God for his guidance in my life. I was afraid to retire because I didn't see how Mark and I would hold things together financially without my income. I also had become so accustomed to the luxuries in life that I found myself having a difficult time giving those up. I remember one night while I was praying I had a feeling that God wanted me to retire. I said, "Okay, God, I really think that you are leading me toward retirement. That probably means that I won't be able to afford some of the clothes and nice things that I have been able to buy. I probably will never have another Longaberger basket, but that's okay. I really feel that you are leading me toward retirement and I want to be in the center of your will, so even if I don't ever get another Longaberger basket that's alright with me." I was comfortable with this decision, but I knew that I would need to sacrifice a lot of things in order to go where I believed God was leading. There was no doubt that God had been sending me subtle messages that I needed to focus my attention on other, more important things at this stage in my life.

My job was taking up so much time that I didn't have time to do anything else. I felt like I was trying to serve two masters and I knew this was a sin. I knew God didn't place me on earth just to earn a paycheck. I knew he wanted to use me to lead others toward a personal relationship with him, and I knew he wanted me to be active in the lives of my family members. There was no doubt that God was leading me to an early retirement, so I asked him to open the doors for me so that I could take an early retirement from General Motors. Soon after I decided to retire, General Motors offered a new early retirement package. I had never before qualified for any of the packages that General Motors offered.

I was either too young or didn't have enough years of tenure to fit into the other retirement packages. I found, however, that I could qualify for the retirement package that was currently being offered. I took this as an unmistakable sign that God was opening the doors for me. Surprisingly, I asked God for another sign just so I could be sure that I was doing his will. When I applied for the early retirement package my boss was pretty upset with me. I wasn't one of the people targeted with this retirement package and he didn't want to lose me. He tried to discourage me on several occasions from taking the early retirement, but I went ahead and applied for the package that was being offered. I don't think there was anything that would have dissuaded me from my decision.

The amazing thing is that when I walked out of the office on my last day of employment there was a beautiful rainbow in the sky. I took this as God's sign that I was in the center of his will and that I had made the right decision. I had no doubt that God would take care of me and I didn't have anything to worry about. The other amazing thing is that on the day I retired from General Motors I received a gift from one of my coworkers. The gift was a Longaberger basket. I had never told anyone about my prayer to God when I was contemplating an early retirement. I had never before received a Longaberger basket as a gift. I took this as another sign from God that he would provide a few of the luxuries that I had come to enjoy. On Christmas of this same year my sister Jackie gave me a Longaberger basket as a gift. I had never received Longaberger baskets as gifts, and I had just received two baskets the same year I retired from General Motors.

Mathew 6:25-34 says the following:

Therefore I tell you, do not worry about your life,

*what you will eat or drink; or about your body,
what you will wear. Is not life more important
than food, and the body more important than
clothes? Look at the birds in the air; they do not
sow or reap or store away in barns, and yet your
heavenly Father feeds them. Are you not much
more valuable than they? Who of you by worrying
can add a single hour to his life? And why do you
worry about clothes? See how the lilies of the field
grow. They do not labor or spin. Yet I tell you that
not even Solomon in all his splendor was dressed
like one of these. If that is how God clothes the
grass of the field, which is here today and
tomorrow is thrown into the fire, will he not much
more clothe you, O you of little faith? So do not
worry, saying, "What shall we eat?" or "What
shall we drink?" or "What shall we wear?" For the
pagans run after all these things, and your
heavenly Father knows that you need them. But
seek first his kingdom and his righteousness, and
all these things will be given to you as well.
Therefore do not worry about tomorrow, for
tomorrow will worry about itself. Each day has
enough trouble of its own.*

God had shown me the signs necessary for me to be sure
that I was doing the right thing. In addition, he let me know
that I was in the center of his will and he would provide for
me. I have no doubt that God was showing me that he
understood what was important to me and would provide for
me. He let me know that he would provide some of the
luxuries that I was accustomed to while Mark and I were both
working.

Neither Mark nor I have quite as many luxuries as we had when we were both working for General Motors, but I know that every luxury I have comes from God and I thoroughly enjoy them. I honestly think I get much more enjoyment out of the fewer luxuries I have now than I ever got from all of the luxuries that Mark and I had when we were both working for General Motors. In addition, Mark and I lead much less stressful lives.

We are able to find time to spend together and we no longer feel that we're servants to our jobs. We both have time to take part in the activities that we believe are important in life. I have never regretted my decision to take an early retirement. I have come to understand that I was a little wasteful when Mark and I were both working. I have found that Mark and I can get by with much less income than I ever thought possible. God has done a great job educating Mark and me on how to live on the income that he provides.

There were a few other things that were pretty amazing about my decision to take an early retirement. At the same time I was contemplating my retirement, Debbie was contemplating leaving her job. She felt that she wanted to take the time to have a closer relationship with God. She was also finding that her job was conflicting with her ability to seek a more fulfilling relationship with God. She had been praying about this and believed she was being led to quit her job. The interesting thing is that on the day Debbie left her job in Wisconsin she also saw a rainbow in the sky.

Debbie and I both took these as unmistakable signs from God that we had made the correct decision, and were in the center of his will.

Neither Debbie nor I knew it at the time but Debbie would suffer from brain cancer and die only a few years after her retirement. I think God led Debbie and me to leave our jobs so that we would be in a position to spend some quality time together before her death. Paula was also diagnosed with cancer during this same timeframe. I am sure that I would never have had the opportunity to spend the last two years of Debbie's life in close contact with her had I not taken an early retirement. I would have never had the opportunity to travel to Tennessee to visit with Paula so many times in the hospital when she was dying of cancer. I might not have had the opportunity to witness to Paula in Tennessee had I still been working a full-time job.

Prior to my retirement I was driving a car that was about six years old. I loved the car but I was starting to have some concerns about how reliable it was. The car had quite a few miles on it because I had taken it on several trips from Michigan to Wisconsin to be with Debbie when she was dying. On a few occasions I had trouble getting the car started. I didn't want to buy a new car because of my retirement and the fact that money was tight. Mark and I both turned this matter over to God through prayer. We prayed for God to find a way to provide a dependable car for me.

Our son-in-law is a car salesman. Mark asked him to look for a car. Initially he had discouraging news. He knew it would be very difficult to find a car for the amount of money we wanted to spend, but he told us he would see what he could do. After hearing the news, I told Mark to just forget about getting me a new car. I told him that I would be fine with my old car because I really didn't think there was any way we could afford a new car. A few weeks later the dealership took delivery of a car that another dealer had ordered. The ordering dealership was supposed to have sent someone over to take delivery of the car. Our son-in-law had been calling the ordering dealer for several weeks, asking him to pick up the car, but the dealer didn't want to take possession of the car for some reason. He finally called Mark and asked him if he would be interested in buying the car.

The car's specifications were very odd. The car was a Chevrolet Lumina with virtually no options. The only option that had been ordered on the car was a driver's side power seat. He knew the car would be hard to sell on his dealer's lot with the odd set of options, and he knew Mark and I were looking for a car that we could purchase at the right price. As a result, he called Mark and asked him if he would be interested in purchasing this car. It turned out that Mark was able to purchase the car for the exact amount of money that we were comfortable paying.

The only option on the car, the driver's side power seat, was actually an important option for me. I'm very short and it's difficult for me to drive a car that doesn't have a power seat. Unbelievably, the only option that had been ordered on the car was the option that was most important to me! Mark and I decided to purchase the car. It turned out that shortly after we purchased the car Paula took a turn for the worse in Tennessee. She began bleeding internally and I had to make the trip to Tennessee without Mark because he couldn't get out of work on such short notice. I think God knew that I needed a dependable car to make that trip to Tennessee and I think he made it possible for Mark and me to purchase this car.

He knew that Mark and I didn't have a lot of money to spend on a new car and he opened the doors that enabled me to purchase a car that matched my needs perfectly. Mark has since told me that when we were praying for this car he had a feeling that my next car was going to be white. The car that we purchased from Matt was a white Chevrolet Lumina. Mark told me that as soon as he heard the car was white he knew God had provided the car for us.

I know God led Debbie and me to leave our jobs in order to allow us the opportunity to spend some quality time together before she passed away. Not only that, but I have no doubt in my mind that God supplied the car I used to make several trips to Tennessee to visit with Paula as she was dying. I thank God that I had the opportunity to spend time with them before they died. It's amazing how everything seemed to fall into place. He truly is an amazing God and truly does supply our every need in a miraculous manner.

God also cured me of my irrational fear of driving during this period in my life in order to enable me to make several long trips on my own to Wisconsin and Tennessee. Mark was unable to come with me on many of the trips, so it was important that I be able to make them on my own. If I had still been bound by the irrational fear of driving, I don't think I could have made these trips on my own. I can't say enough about how God worked in my life during this timeframe. He has shown me time and time again that he is a loving and caring God and that he provides all of our needs.

GOD'S CALLING

It's important to understand that God has charged Christians with a very important job. Jesus provided this "great commission" to his disciples. Acts 22:15 (NLT) says, "You are to take this message everywhere, telling the whole world what you have seen and heard."

In addition, Jesus empowered his followers to do exactly what he was asking them to do.

John 14:12-14 (NLT) says, "The truth is, anyone who believes in me will do the same works I have done, and even greater works, because I am going to be with the Father. You can ask for anything in my name, and I will do it, because the work of the Son brings glory to the Father. Yes, ask anything in my name, and I will do it."

This verse is amazing! What Jesus is telling us is that, through his mercy and faith, he has provided the ability to do the same acts that he was performing – including healings and miracles!

Once we become Christians we cannot ignore this "great commission." There have been numerous debates about the ability to receive our salvation through our works and whether or not the works we perform are required for our salvation. I believe that we do not receive salvation through our works. Our salvation is granted only through the blood of Jesus and the mercy of God. The Bible says the following:

A good tree cannot bring forth evil fruit, neither

> *can a corrupt tree bring forth good fruit. Every tree that bringeth not forth good fruit is hewn down, and cast into the fire. Wherefore by their fruits ye shall know them. "Not everyone that saith unto me, 'Lord, Lord,' shall enter into the kingdom of heaven but he that doeth the will of my Father, which is in heaven. Many will say to me in that day, 'Lord, Lord, have we not prophesied in thy name? And in thy name have cast out devils? And in thy name done many wonderful works?' And then will I profess unto them, 'I never knew you: depart from me, ye that work iniquity.'" (Matt. 7:18-23 KJV)*

This verse shows that we cannot enter into heaven through the performance of works. We must acquire salvation through the blood of Jesus. I don't believe that, once we have truly been saved, that we can ever lose our salvation unless we renounce it. I do believe, however, that once we truly become saved, through the blood of Jesus, that our entire being changes. We will perform good works simply as a result of truly being saved. We can never "earn" or "lose" our salvation through works. The Bible makes it clear that we have all fallen short of the glory of God.

I believe that a person who has truly been saved will perform good works simply as a result of receiving his or her salvation. James 2:14-18, 20 (NLT) says the following:

> *Dear brothers and sisters, what's the use of saying you have faith if you don't prove it by your actions? That kind of faith can't save anyone. Suppose you see a brother or sister who needs food or clothing, and you say, "Well, good-bye and God bless you;*

> *stay warm and eat well" – but then you don't give*
> *that person any food or clothing. What good does*
> *that do? So you see, it isn't enough just to have*
> *faith. Faith that doesn't show itself by good deeds*
> *is no faith at all – it is dead and useless. Now*
> *someone may argue, "Some people have faith;*
> *others have good deeds." I say, "I can't see your*
> *faith if you don't have good deeds, but I will show*
> *you my faith through my good deeds." Fool! When*
> *will you ever learn that faith that does not result*
> *in good deeds is useless?*

This verse indicates that the works that we perform are important and are not ignored by God. The verse doesn't say that works are required for salvation but does point out that a Christian displays his or her faith through good works. The Bible makes it pretty clear that Christians will perform good works and bear good fruit.

The Bible also provides some clear warnings to those who fail to acknowledge Jesus while they are on this earth. "If anyone acknowledges me publicly here on earth, I will openly acknowledge that person before my Father in heaven. But if anyone denies me here on earth, I will deny that person before my Father in heaven" (Matt. 10:32-33 NLT).

"If a person is ashamed of me and my message, I, the Son of Man, will be ashamed of that person when I return in my glory and in the glory of the Father and the holy angels" (Luke 9:26 NLT).

If we profess to be Christians we MUST openly profess knowing Jesus and believing in his message! If we fail to do this then we have been warned about how we will be dealt with on the Day of Judgment.

My life has been blessed. I have been witness to numerous miraculous events and healings. This book documents most of those events. I have fostered a close relationship with God through countless hours of prayer, spending time reading God's word, and actively getting involved in church. I have also tried to be obedient to the calling of God — even when it seemed, at times, that he was asking me to do something crazy.

Many of the miraculous events that I have had the opportunity to witness have come during my most active times in church. As a result, I think it's very important that Christians remain active in church and that they take on active roles. I believe an active church life presents many opportunities for Christians to see how God works. If we fail to have an active church life we have fewer opportunities for fellowship with other Christians. In addition, we have fewer opportunities available for God to work within our lives and reveal his glory to us.

W H Y I
B E L I E V E

My life has been touched in so many ways by the direct hand of God. I have shared these moments in my life with you in this book so that you may also know that there is a God. He is at work in the world today and he still performs miracles for those who believe in him. One of the reasons I believe in God is simply because I have felt his direct presence in my life. It's hard to disbelieve when you have felt and witnessed God in a very personal way. There are other reasons, though, that I want to share with you.

THE FULFILLMENT OF PROPHECIES WITHIN THE OLD AND NEW TESTAMENT:

It is the very existence of the Old Testament of the Bible that provides the basis for the proof that Jesus is who he claimed to be — your savior and the Son of God. The Old Testament is a book of historical facts, NOT MYTHS. The Old Testament was written over the course of many centuries. The most important prophesies contained in the Old Testament concerned the life, crucifixion, and resurrection of Jesus. The book was completed long before Jesus was born, and yet the authors of the Old Testament documented his life in explicit detail. The book contains incredible prophecies about every aspect of the ministry of Jesus. These prophesies were written by different authors in different periods of history and yet, when pieced together like some grand puzzle, they establish an unmistakable depiction of the ministry of Jesus exactly as it unfolded.

It is a true miracle that this collection of different authors within different historical contexts could have produced such a complete and astoundingly accurate picture of Jesus. This proves that, while there were many men who helped write the Old Testament, the book itself was authored by the hand of God. The following are samples of the prophecies and foreshadowing events that are included in the Old Testament and center around the ministry of Jesus:

In the Old Testament

Malachi 3:1
> [1] *"See, I will send my messenger, who will prepare the way before me. Then suddenly the Lord you are seeking will come to his temple; the messenger of the covenant, whom you desire, will come," says the LORD Almighty.*

Malachi 4:5
> [1] *See, I will send you the prophet Elijah before that great and dreadful day of the LORD comes.*

In the New Testament

Matthew 3:1-3
> [1] *In those days John the Baptist came, preaching in the Desert of Judea* [2] *and saying, "Repent, for the kingdom of heaven is near."* [3] *This is he who was spoken of through the prophet Isaiah: "A voice of one calling in the desert, 'Prepare the way for the Lord, make straight paths for him.'"*

In the Old Testament

Isaiah 7:13, 14

> [13] *Then Isaiah said, "Hear now, you house of David! Is it not enough to try the patience of men? Will you try the patience of my God also?* [14] *Therefore the Lord himself will give you a sign: The virgin will be with child and will give birth to a son, and will call him Immanuel."*

In the New Testament

Matthew 1:23

> [23] *"The virgin will be with child and will give birth to a son, and they will call him Emanuel"* — *which means, "God with us."*

In the Old Testament

Isaiah 35:5, 6

> [5] *Then will the eyes of the blind be opened and the ears of the deaf unstopped.* [6] *Then will the lame leap like a deer, and the mute tongue shout for joy. Water will gush forth in the wilderness and streams in the desert.*

In the New Testament

Matthew 11:5

> [5] *The blind receive sight, the lame walk, those who have leprosy are cured, the deaf hear, the dead are raised, and the good news is preached to the poor.*

In the Old Testament

Isaiah 53

¹*Who has believed our message and to whom has the arm of the LORD been revealed?* ²*He grew up before him like a tender shoot, and like a root out of dry ground. He had no beauty or majesty to attract us to him, nothing in his appearance that we should desire him.* ³*He was despised and rejected by men, a man of sorrows, and familiar with suffering. Like one from whom men hide their faces he was despised, and we esteemed him not.* ⁴*Surely he took up our infirmities and carried our sorrows, yet we considered him stricken by God, smitten by him, and afflicted.* ⁵*But he was pierced for our transgressions, he was crushed for our iniquities; the punishment that brought us peace was upon him, and by his wounds we are healed.* ⁶*We all, like sheep, have gone astray, each of us has turned to his own way; and the LORD has laid on him the iniquity of us all.* ⁷*He was oppressed and afflicted, yet he did not open his mouth; he was led like a lamb to the slaughter, and as a sheep before her shearers is silent, so he did not open his mouth.* ⁸*By oppression and judgment he was taken away. And who can speak of his descendants? For he was cut off from the land of the living; for the transgression of my people he was stricken.* ⁹*He was assigned a grave with the wicked, and with the rich in his death, though he had done no violence, nor was any deceit in his mouth.* ¹⁰*Yet it was the LORD's will to crush him and cause him to suffer, and though the LORD makes his life a guilt offering, he will see his offspring and prolong his days, and the will*

of the LORD will prosper in his hand. ¹¹*After the*
suffering of his soul, he will see the light of life and
be satisfied; by his knowledge my righteous servant
will justify many, and he will bear their iniquities.
¹²*Therefore I will give him a portion among the*
great, and he will divide the spoils with the strong,
because he poured out his life unto death, and was
numbered with the transgressors. For he bore the
sin of many, and made intercession for the
transgressors.

In the Old Testament

Micah 5:2-5

²*"But you, Bethlehem Ephrathah, though you are*
small among the clans of Judah, out of you will
come for me one who will be ruler over Israel,
whose origins are from of old, from ancient times."
³*Therefore Israel will be abandoned until the time*
when she who is in labor gives birth and the rest of
his brothers return to join the Israelites. ⁴*He will*
stand and shepherd his flock in the strength of the
LORD, in the majesty of the name of the LORD
his God. And they will live securely, for then his
greatness will reach to the ends of the earth.

⁵*And he will be their peace. When the Assyrian*
invades our land and marches through our
fortresses, we will raise against him seven
shepherds, even eight leaders of men.

In the New Testament

Matthew 2:1

> [1]*After Jesus was born in Bethlehem in Judea, during the time of King Herod, Magi from the east came to Jerusalem.*

Luke 2:15

> [15]*When the angels had left them and gone into heaven, the shepherds said to one another, "Let's go to Bethlehem and see this thing that has happened, which the Lord has told us about."*

In the Old Testament

Psalms 78:2

> [2]*I will open my mouth in parables, I will utter hidden things, things from of old.*

In the Old Testament

Zechariah 9:9

> [9]*Rejoice greatly, O Daughter of Zion! Shout, Daughter of Jerusalem! See, your king comes to you, righteous and having salvation, gentle and riding on a donkey, on a colt, the foal of a donkey. – Jesus' entry into Jerusalem riding upon a donkey.*

In the New Testament

Matthew 21:1-9

> [1]*As they approached Jerusalem and came to Bethphage on the Mount of Olives, Jesus sent two disciples, [2]saying to them, "Go to the village ahead of you, and at once you will find a donkey tied there, with her colt by her. Untie them and bring*

them to me. ³*If anyone says anything to you, tell him that the Lord needs them, and he will send them right away."*

⁴*This took place to fulfill what was spoken through the prophet:* ⁵*"Say to the Daughter of Zion, 'See, your king comes to you, gentle and riding on a donkey, on a colt, the foal of a donkey.'"* ⁶*The disciples went and did as Jesus had instructed them.* ⁷*They brought the donkey and the colt, placed their cloaks on them, and Jesus sat on them.* ⁸*A very large crowd spread their cloaks on the road, while others cut branches from the trees and spread them on the road.* ⁹*The crowds that went ahead of him and those that followed shouted, "Hosanna to the Son of David!" "Blessed is he who comes in the name of the Lord!" "Hosanna in the highest!"*

In the Old Testament

Psalms 118:22

²²*The stone the builders rejected has become the capstone;*

In the New Testament

Matthew 27:34

⁴²*Jesus said to them, "Have you never read in the Scriptures: 'The stone the builders rejected has become the capstone.'"*

Mark 12:10

¹⁰*Haven't you read this scripture: "'The stone the builders rejected has become the capstone.'"*

In the Old Testament

Psalms 41:9

>⁹*Even my close friend, whom I trusted, he who shared my bread, has lifted up his heel against me.*
>*– Foretold the betrayal of Jesus Christ by one of his disciples.*

In the New Testament

John 13:18-19

>¹⁸*"I am not referring to all of you; I know those I have chosen. But this is to fulfill the scripture: 'He who shares my bread has lifted up his heel against me.'* ¹⁹*"I am telling you now before it happens, so that when it does happen you will believe that I am He."*

In the Old Testament

Zechariah 11:12-13

>¹²*I told them, "If you think it best, give me my pay; but if not, keep it." So they paid me thirty pieces of silver.* ¹³*And the LORD said to me, "Throw it to the potter" — the handsome price at which they priced me! So I took the thirty pieces of silver and threw them into the house of the LORD to the potter.*

In the New Testament

Matthew 26:15-16

>¹⁵*and asked, "What are you willing to give me if I hand him over to you?" So they counted out for*

him thirty silver coins. [16] *From then on Judas watched for an opportunity to hand him over.*

Matthew 27:3-10

[3] *When Judas, who had betrayed him, saw that Jesus was condemned, he was seized with remorse and returned the thirty silver coins to the chief priests and the elders.* [4] *"I have sinned," he said, "for I have betrayed innocent blood." "What is that to us?" they replied. "That's your responsibility."* [5] *So Judas threw the money into the temple and left. Then he went away and hanged himself.* [6] *The chief priests picked up the coins and said, "It is against the law to put this into the treasury, since it is blood money."* [7] *So they decided to use the money to buy the potter's field as a burial place for foreigners.* [8] *That is why it has been called the Field of Blood to this day.*

[9] *Then what was spoken by Jeremiah the prophet was fulfilled: "They took the thirty silver coins, the price set on him by the people of Israel,* [10] *and they used them to buy the potter's field, as the Lord commanded me."*

In the Old Testament

Psalms 22:16

[16] *Dogs have surrounded me; a band of evil men has encircled me, they have pierced my hands and my feet.*

In the Old Testament

Psalms 22:18

[18] *They divide my garments among them and cast lots for my clothing.*

In the New Testament

Matthew 27:35
[35] *When they had crucified him, they divided up his clothes by casting lots.*

In the Old Testament

Psalms 22:7, 8
[7] *All who see me mock me; they hurl insults, shaking their heads:* [8] *"He trusts in the LORD; let the LORD rescue him. Let him deliver him, since he delights in him."*

In the New Testament

Matthew 27:43
[43] *He trusts in God. Let God rescue him now if he wants him, for he said, 'I am the Son of God.'"*

In the Old Testament

Psalms 69:21
[21] *They put gall in my food and gave me vinegar for my thirst.*

In the New Testament

Matthew 27:34
[34] *There they offered Jesus wine to drink, mixed with gall; but after tasting it, he refused to drink it.*

In the Old Testament

Psalms 22:1

> [1]*My God, my God, why have you forsaken me?
> Why are you so far from saving me, so far from the
> words of my groaning?*

In the New Testament

Mark 15:34

> [34]*And at the ninth hour Jesus cried out in a loud
> voice, "Eloi, Eloi, lama sabachthani?" — which
> means, "My God, my God, why have you forsaken
> me?"*

In the Old Testament

Zechariah 12:10

> [10]*"And I will pour out on the house of David and
> the inhabitants of Jerusalem a spirit of grace and
> supplication. They will look on me, the one they
> have pierced, and they will mourn for him as one
> mourns for an only child, and grieve bitterly for
> him as one grieves for a firstborn son."*

In the New Testament

John 19:34-37

> [34]*Instead, one of the soldiers pierced Jesus' side with
> a spear, bringing a sudden flow of blood and water.*
> [35]*The man who saw it has given testimony, and his
> testimony is true. He knows that he tells the truth,
> and he testifies so that you also may believe.*
> [36]*These things happened so that the scripture*

would be fulfilled: "Not one of his bones will be broken," [37] *and, as another scripture says, "They will look on the one they have pierced."*

The pages of the Old Testament describe the entire ministry of Jesus, yet the period of time between the writing of the Old Testament and the New Testament is about 400 years. How can a book dating 400 years prior to the start of the New Testament foretell just about every event in the ministry of Jesus if God didn't author it? If you take a look at these prophesies together it becomes clear that they could be attributed to only one man in history.

It has been argued that Jesus could have fulfilled the prophecies foretold in the Old Testament simply because he knew them. The argument states that Jesus could have caused events to happen in order to make it appear that he was the promised Messiah. I would argue, however, that this is ridiculous. It is a fact that Jesus knew the prophesies of the Old Testament very well but it would have been impossible for any man to have forced the fulfillment of many of those prophesies. For instance, how could Jesus have made sure John the Baptist was there to prepare the way for him before he was born? How could Jesus have made sure he was born in the house of David by a virgin? How could Jesus have set the payment amount for his betrayal at 30 pieces of silver? How could he have any control over how the Jewish authority used the blood money to purchase the potter's field? How could Jesus have made sure people drew lots for his garments? How could he have assured they would give him vinegar to drink? For that matter, how could Jesus have selected the method of his execution? He certainly hadn't done anything to deserve crucifixion and yet that was the method of execution that was chosen for him.

The LIVES *and* CHARACTER *of the* EARLY APOSTLES:

The early apostles had no selfish motives. They had nothing personal to gain and everything to lose for spreading the message of the resurrection of Jesus. The apostles were men of utmost character, chosen by the hand of God. The early apostles lived simple lives. They didn't get rich or attain any profit from spreading their message. Furthermore, they endured great ridicule and persecution. Virtually all of the apostles were ultimately killed and suffered horrible deaths as martyrs. Through all of this persecution, and with very little worldly wealth to gain, they never renounced their faith in the message they were spreading. This message is documented in the New Testament of the Bible. If you believe no other non-fiction book, you should believe this one because the authors of the New Testament paid a heavy price to bring this message to you.

Look at Paul's life as an example. Paul (as Saul) was totally devoted to the Jewish faith. He was present at the stoning of Stephen and cheered the crowd on as they murdered Stephen. He even looked after their coats while the stoning took place.

Acts 7:54-59 says:

> [54] *When they heard this, they were furious and gnashed their teeth at him.* [55] *But Stephen, full of*

the Holy Spirit, looked up to heaven and saw the glory of God, and Jesus standing at the right hand of God. ⁵⁶"Look," he said, "I see heaven open and the Son of Man standing at the right hand of God."

⁵⁷At this they covered their ears and, yelling at the top of their voices, they all rushed at him, ⁵⁸dragged him out of the city and began to stone him. Meanwhile, the witnesses laid their clothes at the feet of a young man named Saul. ⁵⁹While they were stoning him, Stephen prayed, "Lord Jesus, receive my spirit." ⁶⁰Then he fell on his knees and cried out, "Lord, do not hold this sin against them." When he had said this, he fell asleep.

Paul (as Saul) spent his aggressions persecuting and killing Christians. After the Holy Spirit revealed himself to Saul, however, he became completely devoted to spreading the Christian message. Here is Paul's own account, as told in the Bible in Acts 22:1-24:

¹"Brothers and fathers, listen now to my defense." ²When they heard him speak to them in Aramaic, they became very quiet.

³Then Paul said: "I am a Jew, born in Tarsus of Cilicia, but brought up in this city. Under Gamaliel I was thoroughly trained in the law of our fathers and was just as zealous for God as any of you are today. ⁴I persecuted the followers of this Way to their death, arresting both men and women and throwing them into prison, ⁵as also the high priest and all the Council can testify. I even obtained letters from them to their brothers in

Damascus, and went there to bring these people as prisoners to Jerusalem to be punished.

[6] "About noon as I came near Damascus, suddenly a bright light from heaven flashed around me. [7] I fell to the ground and heard a voice say to me, 'Saul! Saul! Why do you persecute me?'

[8] "'Who are you, Lord?' I asked.

"'I am Jesus of Nazareth, whom you are persecuting,' he replied. [9] My companions saw the light, but they did not understand the voice of him who was speaking to me.

[10] "'What shall I do, Lord?' I asked.

[11] "Get up," the Lord said, 'and go into Damascus. There you will be told all that you have been assigned to do.' My companions led me by the hand into Damascus, because the brilliance of the light had blinded me.

[12] "A man named Ananias came to see me. He was a devout observer of the law and highly respected by all the Jews living there. [13] He stood beside me and said, 'Brother Saul, receive your sight!' And at that very moment I was able to see him.

[14] "Then he said: 'The God of our fathers has chosen you to know his will and to see the Righteous One and to hear words from his mouth. [15] You will be his witness to all men of what you have seen and heard. [16] And now what are you waiting for? Get up, be baptized and wash your sins away, calling on his name.'

[17] "When I returned to Jerusalem and was praying at the temple, I fell into a trance [18] and saw the Lord speaking. 'Quick!' he said to me. 'Leave Jerusalem immediately, because they will not

accept your testimony about me.'

[19] *"'Lord,' I replied, 'these men know that I went from one synagogue to another to imprison and beat those who believe in you.* [20] *And when the blood of your martyr Stephen was shed, I stood there giving my approval and guarding the clothes of those who were killing him.'*

[21] *"Then the Lord said to me, 'Go; I will send you far away to the Gentiles.'"*

[22] *The crowd listened to Paul until he said this. Then they raised their voices and shouted, "Rid the earth of him! He's not fit to live!"*

[23] *As they were shouting and throwing off their cloaks and flinging dust into the air,* [24] *the commander ordered Paul to be taken into the barracks. He directed that he be flogged and questioned in order to find out why the people were shouting at him like this.*

He endured terrible things as he spread the message of Jesus. He was stoned to the point that people thought he was dead, only to get up and return to the city to preach! Acts 14:19-23 testifies to this:

[19] *Then some Jews came from Antioch and Iconium and won the crowd over. They stoned Paul and dragged him outside the city, thinking he was dead.* [20] *But after the disciples had gathered around him, he got up and went back into the city. The next day he and Barnabas left for Derbe.*

[21] *They preached the good news in that city and won a large number of disciples. Then they returned to Lystra, Iconium and Antioch,*

> [22] *strengthening the disciples and encouraging them to remain true to the faith. "We must go through many hardships to enter the kingdom of God," they said.* [23] *Paul and Barnabas appointed elders for them in each church and, with prayer and fasting, committed them to the Lord, in whom they had put their trust.*

Paul had been shipwrecked three times, arrested numerous times, and stoned and ridiculed to the point that people thought he was dead. How many other people facing such persecution and setbacks would wonder, *Is God really with me?* But Paul never doubted his purpose. He knew, once he had come face-to-face with the Holy Spirit on the road to Damascus, that his one purpose in life was to spread the message of the resurrection of Jesus. He carried out this purpose no matter what obstacles stood in his path. That's true conviction! It must have been a life-changing event for Paul (and it certainly was).

One brief encounter with the Holy Spirit on the road to Damascus completely changed Paul's life and he became totally committed to spreading the message of Christianity all over the known world no matter what the personal cost. He endured terrible persecution and was ultimately martyred for spreading the message of the resurrection of Jesus. Only one thing can explain this — Paul's encounter with the Holy Spirit made him believe beyond a shadow of a doubt that Jesus was the promised Messiah that he had, up to that point, rejected.

Besides Paul, Peter also faced terrible persecution and imprisonment for spreading the message of Jesus. Ultimately Peter was executed (crucified upside down) for his beliefs. Peter is the same apostle who had denied knowing Jesus three times prior to his death. After Jesus died on the cross, was resurrected from the dead, and had reappeared to his apostles, Peter had a renewed conviction to spread the message of Jesus. Peter went to the grave and never again renounced knowing Jesus. He had lived with Jesus, had seen the miracles Jesus performed, he witnessed the crucifixion and resurrection, and had been visited by the Holy Spirit.

If Peter ever doubted that Jesus was the savior, he certainly had plenty of motivation and time to renounce his beliefs. Peter never did — he faced persecution, imprisonment, and a horrible death as a martyr and continued to spread the message of Jesus.

There is no stronger evidence that Jesus is who he claimed to be than the life story of his earliest apostles.

The
REQUIREMENTS
of SALVATION

Many people argue many things about what is required for salvation. I've heard some people say that they don't believe God would ever send a "good" person to hell. Some people say that you can earn your way into heaven. The Bible, however, doesn't support these arguments. Perhaps one of the best passages to look at in the Bible regarding the requirements for salvation is Luke 23:32-43:

> [32] *Two other men, both criminals, were also led out with him to be executed.* [33] *When they came to the place called the Skull, there they crucified him, along with the criminals — one on his right, the other on his left.* [34] *Jesus said, "Father, forgive them, for they do not know what they are doing." And they divided up his clothes by casting lots.*
> [35] *The people stood watching, and the rulers even sneered at him. They said, "He saved others; let him save himself if he is the Christ of God, the Chosen One."*
> [36] *The soldiers also came up and mocked him. They offered him wine vinegar* [37] *and said, "If you are the king of the Jews, save yourself."*
> [38] *There was a written notice above him, which*

read: THIS IS THE KING OF THE JEWS.
[39] *One of the criminals who hung there hurled insults at him: "Aren't you the Christ? Save yourself and us!"*
[40] *But the other criminal rebuked him. "Don't you fear God," he said, "since you are under the same sentence?* [41] *We are punished justly, for we are getting what our deeds deserve. But this man has done nothing wrong."*
[42] *Then he said, "Jesus, remember me when you come into your kingdom."*
[43] *Jesus answered him, "I tell you the truth, today you will be with me in paradise."*

From this passage in the Bible it is clear that we can't earn our salvation through works. Both of the men hanging on either side of Jesus were criminals. Neither of them would have done anything previously in their life that would have been considered good enough for them to "earn" their way into Heaven. This was a deathbed salvation. These criminals who were hanging alongside Jesus wouldn't have had the opportunity to "earn" their way into Heaven — they were being crucified! What seems to be important from these Bible passages is that the criminal who received his salvation recognizes that he is a sinner, because he says, "We are punished justly, for we are getting what our deeds deserve." He also calls upon Jesus for his salvation when he says, "Jesus, remember me when you come into your kingdom." It is apparent from that statement that this criminal really believed that Jesus was the son of God and had the power to cleanse his sins. Those of you who make the argument that God would never send a "good" person to hell should remember the words of the Apostle's Creed. The creed reads as follows:

I believe in God, the Father Almighty, Maker of heaven and earth, and in Jesus Christ, his only begotten Son, our Lord who was conceived by the Holy Ghost, born of the Virgin Mary, suffered under Pontius Pilate; was crucified, dead and buried. He descended into hell. The third day he rose again from the dead. He ascended into heaven, and sits at the right hand of God the Father Almighty. From thence he shall come to judge the quick and the dead.
I believe in the Holy Ghost. I believe in the holy Catholic Church, the communion of saints, the forgiveness of sins, the resurrection of the body, and the life everlasting. Amen."

This is the basic creed of reformed churches, and is most familiarly known as the "Apostle's Creed." It received this title because of its great antiquity. The creed dates from very early times in the Christian church — a half century or so from the last writings of the New Testament. This extremely early creed of the Christian church points out the fact that Jesus died on the cross for your sins. He was dead and buried for three days. HE DESCENDED INTO HELL and was resurrected from the dead and appeared to his apostles.

If God would permit Jesus to descend into Hell for three days, what makes you think he won't send a "good" person to hell? The fact of the matter is that he sent his own son to hell for three days! The Bible makes it pretty clear that we are all sinners and have fallen short of the glory of God. The ONLY way to enter into the presence of God is to accept the salvation that was offered through the sacrifice Jesus made on the cross. Isn't it great to know that we serve a master who was not only willing to suffer a disgraceful and painful death on the cross, but was also willing to go to hell and return for us?

For those of you who doubt the validity of some of the statements in the Apostles' Creed, you should understand that Jesus was God's only son. Jesus had never committed a sin in his life. He was spotless in the sight of God and didn't deserve death. He certainly didn't deserve the horrible means of death that God permitted him to endure. If God would permit his only son (who was without sin) to endure such a painful and horrible death on the cross, what makes you so sure he won't permit a sinner to go to hell for eternity?

A CALL
to ACTION

If you enjoyed reading this book about my Christian testimonial, and your life has been touched in some miraculous manner by Jesus, I would urge you to share your testimony by publishing it in a book or writing a magazine article about the miraculous manner in which Jesus has interacted with you. I am very interested in hearing how God works and would love to read any testimony that you might have time to document. If you have a truly amazing story about how God has interacted in your life feel free to send me an email at SpiritHand@hotmail.com.

I know there are many Christian testimonies that never get documented in writing. Many are never even spoken about in a church service. I think it's incredibly important to communicate and share the awesome ways in which Jesus has worked in the lives of Christians. Not only that, but I think it's of utmost importance to document those stories in a format that can be passed from generation to generation. Christian testimonies are one of the best ways to witness to nonbelievers about the power of Jesus. We, as Christians, need to be advertising the fact that JESUS IS ALIVE AND WELL. He is very active in the world today, and his awesome power is unmatched!

Let's face it, miraculous events are rare and we need to be sharing those events with anyone we encounter. Those miracles have occurred in your lives so that you may bring glory to God's name and witness about him to the ends of the

Earth. They are incredible gifts from God! You should feel truly blessed if Jesus has performed a miracle in your life. They are extremely rare, and many, if not most, Christians may spend their entire lives without ever witnessing a true miracle in their lives. I would urge you to take the time to document your Christian testimonies in writing so that they can be shared with others. Written documents last so much longer than the spoken word. These miraculous testimonies need to be shared and passed from generation to generation.